Beginner's Baking BIBLE

Beginner's *Baking*
BIBLE

130+ Recipes and Techniques for New Bakers

Heather Perine

PHOTOGRAPHY BY HELENE DUJARDIN

ROCKRIDGE
PRESS

Interior and Cover Designer: Stephanie Mautone
Art Producer: Michael Hardgrove
Editor: Jesse Aylen
Production Editor: Chris Gage
Photography © 2019 Helene Dujardin. Food styling by Anna Hampton.
Author photo courtesy of © Emily Brenchley, www.emilybrenchleyphotography.com

ISBN: Print 978-1-64611-137-4 | eBook 978-1-64611-138-1
R0

To Jason, for tasting all the treats
(good and bad) and for washing all those dishes.
Without you, this book would never
have been possible. And to my mom,
for being my biggest cheerleader.

Red Velvet Layer Cake PAGE 134

Contents

Introduction ix

PART I
The Beginner's Building Blocks

1 The Beginning Baker's Kitchen 3

2 Starting Skills 11

PART II
The Recipes

3 A Collection of Cookies 21

4 Basically Brownies and Bars 43

5 Perfect Pies, Galettes, Tarts, and Quiches 59

6 Can't-Fail Quick Breads and Masterful Muffins 95

7 Captivating Cakes and Cupcakes 113

8 Beautiful Breads, Biscuits, and Crackers 139

9 Fantastic Frostings and Glazes 169

Measurement Conversions 185

The Dirty Dozen and The Clean Fifteen™ 186

Resources 187

Index 188

Introduction

When it comes to being in the kitchen, I don't think there is anything more rewarding than baking something from scratch. Baking for someone is the best way I know of to show them I care. We celebrate milestones in our lives—from birthdays to anniversaries—with baked goods or share them to let someone know we are thinking about them. However, as inspiring as baking can be, it can also be intimidating. One thing that seems to scare people away is a fear of having to closely follow a recipe. In cooking, you can throw in a pinch of this or that without a fear of failure. But baking requires reading a recipe, using precise measurements, and applying specific techniques. And, yes, failure can happen. Cookies can fall flat. Cakes can sink. Sometimes breads won't rise. But that's okay, and baking doesn't have to be scary. Baking is a science, after all. Once you get the basics down, you will have eliminated the guesswork and it will be sweet (or savory) success every time.

Growing up, my only baking experience was making the classic cookie recipe we all know from that yellow bag of chocolate chips. I don't come from a long line of chefs, and I haven't attended culinary school; I'm a home baker just like you. I took up—and fell in love with—baking in my early twenties when I took a culinary class. After that, I wanted to learn as much as possible. I read every cookbook I could get my hands on and took every course I could find. The best teacher, however, was simply practicing—and sometimes failing—in my own kitchen. And that's how I know that learning to become a better baker is something anyone can do.

In the *Beginner's Baking Bible*, you will learn how to make an assortment of baked goods that will impress your friends and family, including classic breakfast staples like blueberry muffins and buttermilk biscuits, as well as cookies, cakes, pies, tarts, quiches, and even savory breads. In addition to the recipes themselves, I'll share my best tips and tricks that I've learned through my own missteps, and help you troubleshoot recipes so you can grow your skills as a baker. Baking is something that can be easily learned. You don't need a culinary degree or a "baking gene" to be successful. The best way to learn is by simply getting started.

So, are you ready? Let's get baking!

PART I

The Beginner's Building Blocks

1

The Beginning Baker's Kitchen

To bake a range of delicious confections, you don't need to use fancy gadgets, obscure processes, or hard-to-find ingredients. You will need some basics to get the job done properly, however. In this chapter, I'll share must-have tools and ingredients to stock your kitchen, plus the nice-to-have items for when you're ready to move beyond the basics.

ESSENTIAL EQUIPMENT

It can be tempting to stock your kitchen with every single pan and appliance available—trust me, I know! But, as I've learned over the years, you need only a few essential items to tackle most baking recipes.

Cookware and Bakeware

MUST HAVE

Baking sheets: Flat metal baking sheets are available with a rim or without. I prefer ones with a rim because they can be used to bake cookies, bars, and even cakes. Invest in two so you can rotate batches in and out of the oven.

Baking pans: Baking pans come in a variety of sizes and shapes—most have sides about 2 inches deep. My go-to baking pans are a 9-by-13-inch rectangular pan, an 8-by-8-inch square pan, 8½-by-4½-inch and 9-by-5-inch loaf pans, two 9-inch round cake pans, and a 12-cup cupcake/muffin pan. I recommend aluminum baking pans for their even heating and cooling properties.

Pie dish: I recommend a 9-inch glass pie dish.

NICE TO HAVE

Bundt cake pan: A Bundt pan is a round metal pan with a hole in the middle and uniform ridges up the side.

Tart pan: This 9- or 10-inch round pan has fluted edges and a removable bottom, making it ideal for baking beautiful tarts.

Tools and Utensils

MUST HAVE

Measuring tools: Invest in a set of dry measuring cups, a glass liquid measuring cup, and a set of measuring spoons. Choose metal and glass, as plastic can retain odors and residue.

Mixing tools: A set of mixing bowls (again, metal is best), a silicone spatula, and a wire whisk are essential.

Cooling rack: Baked goods continue to bake once you've removed them from the oven. Proper cooling on a wire rack helps ensure that they don't end up overbaked.

Rolling pin: A wooden rolling pin is essential for pie dough, certain types of cookies, and breads. My favorite is a French rolling pin made of solid wood that is tapered at the ends.

Parchment paper or silicone baking mat: Parchment paper or a reusable silicone baking mat makes cleanup a breeze and keeps cookies from spreading too much.

NICE TO HAVE

Cookie scoop: A cookie scoop ensures that you have evenly sized cookies every time.

Microplane rasp grater: A rasp grater makes zesting citrus and grating fresh nutmeg quick and easy.

Appliances

MUST HAVE

Mixer: Handheld electric mixers with beaters are available in a range of price points and make fast work of creaming butter and sugar for cookies, mixing cake batters, and whipping egg whites.

NICE TO HAVE

Food processor: This makes quick work of assembling pie dough, chopping nuts, and shredding vegetables (like carrots for a carrot cake).

Stand mixer: If you have space in your kitchen and your budget, a stand mixer is a great investment. Thanks to its large capacity and heavy-duty motor, making cakes and cookie dough, whipping egg whites, and kneading bread dough become fast and easy tasks.

ESSENTIAL INGREDIENTS

Just like you don't need fancy equipment to be successful, you don't need exotic or expensive ingredients either. It is important, however, to use quality ingredients. Any of these staple ingredients can easily be found at your local grocery store.

MUST HAVE

Flours: Flour builds structure because it contains proteins that, when hydrated, form gluten. Without gluten, your baked goods would fall apart. All-purpose flour has moderate protein content, making it ideal for many recipes. Bread flour has higher protein content, which gives bread its elasticity. Cake flour has lower protein content, which gives cakes a delicate texture. Store flour in a cool, dry place.

Sugars: Best known as a sweetener, sugar also provides moisture. The most commonly used sugars are granulated white, brown (light or dark), and powdered (confectioner's). Use caution when substituting sugar alternatives, such as honey, because they can affect texture. Store sugar in a cool, dry place.

Fats: Fats are crucial in making baked goods tender and moist and, depending on which type you use, can also add flavor.

Butter (salted and unsalted): Butter is wonderful to use for baking because it provides great flavor. I recommend unsalted butter, partly because the amount of salt in salted butter can vary among brands. If you do opt for salted butter, mindfully reduce the amount of salt in the recipe. Store butter, wrapped, in your refrigerator.

Shortening: Shortening is pure fat and increases the tenderness of baked goods, though it doesn't provide the flavor that butter does. Store shortening on your pantry shelf.

Alternatives: Many recipes call for oil instead of butter or shortening. I recommend using a neutral-tasting oil, such as vegetable or canola oil. Other fats such as lard, coconut oil, or margarine can also be used.

Leavening agents: Leavening agents are what cause your baked goods to rise. There are three different kinds: chemical (baking powder or baking soda), biological (yeast), or physical (air or steam). Chemical and biological leavening agents can expire over time, so test them for a reaction before you start (read ahead to find out how).

Baking powder: They may sound similar, but baking powder and baking soda are not interchangeable. Baking powder is baking soda that's been mixed with an acid. Most baking powders are double acting, meaning they react once when moistened and again when heat is applied. Test baking powder by dropping a bit of hot water into a small spoonful to see if it bubbles.

Baking soda: Baking soda, or bicarbonate of soda, reacts with a recipe's acidic ingredients, such as buttermilk, though it can be used on its own to help leaven a recipe. Before you use that ancient box of baking soda lurking in the cupboard, test it with a drop of vinegar or lemon juice to see if it still bubbles.

Yeast: A must-have ingredient when making bread, yeast is a living organism that eats sugar and releases carbon dioxide. When activating yeast, always use warm liquids (105°F to 110°F). Hot liquids will kill it, and cold liquids will not activate it. Opened packets of yeast should be stored in the refrigerator and used by their expiration date.

NICE TO HAVE

Chocolate: Chocolate comes in many forms and contains varying amounts of sugar. For bars and baking chocolate, the higher the percentage of cocoa, the less sugar it has. So an 80 percent chocolate bar is less sweet than a 60 percent chocolate bar. I use unsweetened cocoa powder in these recipes. As Dutch-processed cocoa doesn't produce the same reaction, it should not be substituted. Chocolate should be stored in a cool, dry place.

Nuts: Nuts bring flavor and texture to many recipes. For added flavor, try roasting them before using. If they aren't in the budget, or if nut allergies are a concern, you can always omit them. Nuts are best stored in your freezer.

A Sense About Salt

Salt is essential in baking. It might seem strange to add salt to a dessert, but it helps enhance other flavors, balance sweetness, strengthen bread dough, and make your baked goods last longer. You may notice some recipes call for salt and others call for kosher salt. What's the difference? Regular salt, or table salt, has smaller granules. Kosher salt has larger granules and may not dissolve as easily. If a recipe calls for kosher salt and you add table salt, you may be adding more salt than the recipe calls for, which will result in oversalting. When a recipe simply calls for salt, use table salt.

PERFECT YOUR PROCESS

Anyone who knows me will tell you that organization is not my strong suit—until it's time to bake. Preparation is essential to making baking enjoyable, so here are my most valuable preparation techniques to help you perfect your process.

Prep it: The French call this *mise en place*, or "everything in its place." Read the recipe in its entirety and organize your ingredients before getting started. Allow butter and eggs to come to room temperature, prep your pans, preheat the oven, and prepare ingredients like roasted and chopped nuts. These steps ensure a smooth process and prevent a frantic rush to the store mid-bake for that one surprise missing ingredient!

Grease it: There's nothing worse than going through all the trouble of baking from scratch only to have your treats stick to the pan. Prepare your pans according to the recipe instructions (by coating them with cooking spray, butter, or butter and flour, or lining them with parchment paper or a silicone baking mat) before you start.

Measure it: Successful baking boils down to accurate measurement, which means using the right equipment for the right process. Although it might be tempting to measure your liquids in your dry measuring cups, you won't get an accurate measurement. Use your glass measuring cup and get down to eye level for the best read.

Separate it: Separating eggs is best done with cold eggs, because the yolk is firmer and less likely to break. Separate eggs one at a time in two small bowls. Crack the egg and transfer the egg back and forth gently between your hands, letting the egg white drip into one bowl. When there is no egg white left in your hand, place the egg yolk into the other bowl.

Mix it: It's tempting to throw everything in the bowl all at once to save a few minutes. Although that's probably how many of us baked when we kids, we know better now. Mix your dry ingredients and wet ingredients separately, then combine them together as directed in the recipe. Be careful not to overmix, which can cause certain baked goods to become tough.

Check it: I've taken my fair share of cakes out of the oven too early, only to have my heart sink just like the center of those cakes. Begin checking for doneness at the earliest listed cook time. To

The Measure Matters

To accurately measure flour, start by stirring up the flour in your container since flour can settle as it sits. Use a spoon to scoop the flour into your dry measuring cup. Do not pack the flour down or tap the sides when measuring, as this can result in using too much flour. Once you have a heaping cup, level it off with a flat edge, like the back of a knife.

When measuring sugar, there's a distinct difference between measuring granulated sugar and brown sugar. For granulated sugar, simply scoop it into the measuring cup and level off. Brown sugar, however, needs to be packed down to get an accurate measure. Using the back of a spoon, press down on the sugar until it is firmly packed into your measuring cup. When you have a heaping cupful, level it off.

test for doneness of cakes and cupcakes, insert a toothpick into the center and look for moist crumbs when you extract it. Every oven is different, so don't blindly trust the time listed: Use your eyes and your nose to judge when your baked good is ready.

Just cool it: Just because you took your baked goods out of the oven doesn't mean you're done. Because baked foods can continue to bake when left in the pan (due to residual heat), be sure to follow the recipe instructions and allow them to cool properly on a cooling rack.

2

Starting Skills

I'm going to let you in on a little secret: You have the potential to be a great baker. All it takes is knowing a few essential techniques and a little practice. In this chapter, I'll share the skills you'll use in this cookbook. By the end, you'll be ready to break out those mixing bowls, roll up your sleeves, and start baking with the best of them.

BAKING TECHNIQUES

Mastering key baking techniques—mixing, folding, creaming, kneading, melting, and more—is easier than you'd expect. Just follow these tips and instructions.

Mixing and Folding

Mixing means to stir the ingredients together until they are combined, and it can be done by hand or with an electric mixer. Folding means to combine the ingredients softly to avoid overmixing.

1. To fold lighter ingredients, such as whipped egg whites or whipped cream, into a denser mixture, such as a batter or a custard, add a small amount of the lighter ingredient to the denser mixture, then use a spatula to cut from side to side through the middle of the bowl.

2. Scrape the spatula toward you along the bottom of the bowl, then gently fold the mixture up over itself. Rotate the bowl and repeat this process until the ingredients are combined. Add the rest of the lighter ingredients and fold until they are fully incorporated.

Creaming Butter and Sugar

Creaming is the process of beating air into butter, which provides structure for baked goods. Sugar is responsible for "punching" holes in the butter and creating air pockets. Always use softened butter. Creaming can be done by hand or with a mixer.

1. Add the sugar to the butter.

2. Mix until the butter has a light color and fluffy texture. If using a mixer, set it at medium speed and mix for 2 to 3 minutes. Be careful to not to overmix, which can result in a dense finished product.

Kneading Dough

Kneading dough helps develop the gluten, which is responsible for the strength and structure of yeasted doughs. The steps here are for kneading by hand, but you can also use a stand mixer fitted with a dough hook attachment—just remember to use the "windowpane test" to check the dough's progress.

1. Shape the dough into a ball. Using the palms of your hands, push the dough down and away from your body.

2. Fold the dough in half, give it a quarter turn, and repeat step 1 until the dough is soft and supple (up to 10 minutes).

3. To check if the dough has been kneaded long enough, conduct the "windowpane test." Remove a piece of dough and stretch it into a thin membrane that you can see through. If the dough tears while stretching, knead it a bit more.

Whipping Egg Whites

Whipping egg whites adds air into the whites to lighten them into a fluffy cloud. Whipped egg whites can be used for meringues or to help cakes rise.

1. Start with clean, dry metal bowls and utensils. Separate the egg whites from the yolks, making sure there is no trace of yolk in the whites, as yolks can prevent the egg whites from whipping up fully.

2. Using an electric mixer, start mixing on low and gradually increase the speed to whip the egg whites to your desired firmness.

3. When the egg whites are properly whipped, soft peaks will hold their shape but will fall over when you lift the beaters from the bowl. Firm peaks will not fall over when you lift the beaters from the bowl.

Cutting Butter into Flour

"Cutting in" means to incorporate butter into flour. It is the key to making tender, flaky pastries, biscuits, and pie crusts. Unless otherwise stated in the recipe, always use cold butter, preferably cut into small cubes. If you don't have a pastry blender, you can also use a food processor for this task, but be sure to pulse the butter into the flour, so as not to overwork the dough.

1. Put the flour and butter into a bowl. Using a pastry blender, cut and blend the butter into the flour.

2. Continue blending until the butter is in pea-size pieces and the texture is pebbly, with small visible pieces of butter coated in flour.

Melting Chocolate

Melting chocolate can be done on the stovetop or in the microwave. Either way, be sure your utensils are completely dry. If water gets into the chocolate, the chocolate can seize.

1. To melt chocolate on the stove, place the chopped chocolate in a double boiler or a heat-proof bowl set over a pot of simmering water. Stir frequently.

2. To melt chocolate in the microwave, place the chocolate in a heat-proof bowl and heat in 30-second intervals. Stir between each interval to prevent burning.

PART II

The Recipes

Raspberry-Almond Thumbprints **PAGE 24**

3

A Collection of Cookies

Easy Sugar Cookies 22

Snickerdoodles 23

Raspberry-Almond Thumbprints 24

Espresso and Chocolate
Chip Shortbread 25

Maple Cookies 26

Coconut Macaroons 27

Soft Molasses Cookies 28

Soft Peanut Butter Cookies 29

Oatmeal Cookies 30

Perfect Chocolate Chip Cookies 31

Pistachio Cookies 32

Pumpkin and White Chocolate
Chip Cookies 33

Chocolate Brownie Cookies 34

Spiced Hot Chocolate Cookies 35

Monster Cookies 36

Red Velvet Chocolate
Chip Cookies 37

Iced Lime Meltaways 38

Glazed Orange Ricotta Cookies 39

Carrot Cake and Oatmeal
Cookie Sandwiches 40

Easy Sugar Cookies

Makes 24 cookies

This cookie recipe is for my dad, who requests sugar cookies for every holiday. Unlike sugar cookie dough that needs to be rolled, chilled, and cut, this dough can be scooped right from the bowl and then baked. *Nut-free*

PREP TIME: 15 minutes
COOK TIME: 12 minutes

3 cups all-purpose flour

1 teaspoon baking powder

¼ teaspoon baking soda

½ teaspoon salt

1 cup (2 sticks) unsalted butter, room temperature

1¼ cups granulated sugar

2 teaspoons vanilla extract

1 large egg, room temperature

½ cup sprinkles (optional)

1. **Preheat the oven.** Preheat the oven to 375°F. Line two baking sheets with parchment paper or silicone baking mats.

2. **Combine the dry ingredients.** In a medium bowl, whisk together the flour, baking powder, baking soda, and salt.

3. **Cream the butter and sugar.** In a large bowl, using an electric mixer, cream the butter and sugar until light and fluffy, about 2 minutes.

4. **Add the vanilla and egg.** Add the vanilla and egg and mix until just combined. Scrape down the bowl as needed.

5. **Add the dry ingredients.** Add the flour mixture and mix at medium-low speed until the dough is evenly moistened. Using a rubber spatula, stir in the sprinkles, if using.

6. **Scoop.** Using a tablespoon, scoop the dough into 1½-inch balls and place them on the baking sheets, leaving about 2 inches between each cookie.

7. **Bake.** Bake for 10 to 12 minutes, or until the edges of the cookies begin to brown. Cool on the baking sheets for 5 minutes. Transfer the cookies to a wire rack to cool completely.

PREPARATION TIP: Instead of adding sprinkles to the dough, pour the sprinkles into a shallow bowl. In step 6, roll each dough ball in the bowl and coat it evenly with the sprinkles, then proceed as directed.

Snickerdoodles

Makes about 24 cookies

Snickerdoodles contain a unique ingredient—cream of tartar—that gives them their slightly tangy flavor and chewy texture. *Nut-free*

PREP TIME: **15 minutes, plus 1 hour to chill**
COOK TIME: **8 minutes**

1 cup (2 sticks) unsalted butter, room temperature

1½ cups granulated sugar

2 large eggs, room temperature

2 teaspoons vanilla extract

2¾ cups all-purpose flour

2 teaspoons cream of tartar

1 teaspoon baking soda

¼ teaspoon salt

5 tablespoons granulated sugar, for topping

5 teaspoons ground cinnamon, for topping

1. **Preheat the oven.** Preheat the oven to 400°F. Line two baking sheets with parchment paper or silicone baking mats.

2. **Combine the wet ingredients.** In a large bowl, using an electric mixer, cream the butter and sugar until light and fluffy, about 2 minutes. Add the eggs, one at a time, mixing well after each addition. Scrape down the bowl as needed. Mix in the vanilla.

3. **Add the dry ingredients.** Mix in the flour, cream of tartar, baking soda, and salt.

4. **Refrigerate the dough.** Refrigerate the dough for at least 1 hour.

5. **Make the topping.** In a small bowl, mix together the sugar and cinnamon for the topping.

6. **Scoop.** Using a tablespoon, scoop the dough into 1½-inch balls and immediately roll each dough ball in the cinnamon-sugar mixture until thoroughly coated. Place the dough balls on the baking sheets, leaving about 2 inches between each cookie.

7. **Bake.** Bake for 8 minutes, or until the tops of the cookies are set. Cool on the baking sheets for 5 minutes. Transfer the cookies to a wire cooling rack to cool completely.

SUBSTITUTION TIP: If you don't have cream of tartar, omit the baking soda and substitute 2 teaspoons of baking powder.

Raspberry-Almond Thumbprints

Makes about 14 cookies

These buttery cookies are made with classic shortbread
dough that gets rolled into a ball before being indented by
your thumb and filled with sweet raspberry jam.

PREP TIME: **10 minutes**
COOK TIME: **17 minutes**

8 tablespoons (1 stick)
    unsalted butter,
    room temperature

⅓ cup granulated sugar

1 egg yolk, room
    temperature

1 teaspoon vanilla extract

½ teaspoon almond
    extract

1 cup plus 2 tablespoons
    all-purpose flour

½ teaspoon salt

3½ teaspoons raspberry
    jam

1. **Preheat the oven.** Preheat the oven to 350°F. Line
two baking sheets with parchment paper or silicone
baking mats.

2. **Cream the butter and sugar.** In a large bowl, using
an electric mixer, cream the butter and sugar until light
and fluffy, about 2 minutes.

3. **Add the egg yolk and extracts.** Add the egg yolk,
mixing until incorporated. Add the vanilla and almond
extract and mix until just combined. Scrape down the
bowl as needed.

4. **Add the dry ingredients.** Add the flour and salt and
mix until just combined.

5. **Shape the cookies.** With your hands, roll the dough
into 1-inch balls and place them on the baking sheets,
leaving about 2 inches between each cookie. Using your
thumb, or the back of a ¼ teaspoon, gently press into
the center of each cookie to make a small well. Fill each
well with ¼ teaspoon of jam.

6. **Bake.** Bake for 15 to 17 minutes, or until the cookies
are light brown on the bottom. Cool on the baking
sheets for 5 minutes. Transfer the cookies to a wire rack
to cool completely.

TROUBLESHOOTING TIP: When creating the well,
lightly flour your thumb or the spoon to prevent sticking.

Espresso and Chocolate Chip Shortbread

Makes 20 cookies

Combining a bold bittersweet espresso punch with rich chocolate that practically melts in your mouth, these shortbread treats are ideal for a midafternoon break or as a snack with your morning latte. *Nut-free*

PREP TIME: 10 minutes, plus 2 hours to chill

COOK TIME: 10 minutes

1 cup (2 sticks) unsalted butter, room temperature

¾ cup granulated sugar

1 teaspoon vanilla extract

2 cups all-purpose flour

½ teaspoon salt

1 tablespoon instant espresso powder

¾ cup miniature semisweet chocolate chips

1. **Cream the butter, sugar, and vanilla.** In a large bowl, using an electric mixer, cream the butter, sugar, and vanilla until light and fluffy, about 2 minutes.

2. **Add the remaining ingredients.** Add the flour, salt, and espresso powder, mixing until just combined. Using a rubber spatula, stir in the chocolate chips.

3. **Refrigerate the dough.** Turn the dough out onto a large piece of plastic wrap and shape it into a log about 1½-inch thick. Tightly wrap the dough and refrigerate for 2 hours, or until firm.

4. **Bake.** About 15 minutes before baking, preheat the oven to 375°F. Line two baking sheets with parchment paper or silicone baking mats. Unwrap the dough and cut it into ¼-inch-thick slices. Bake for 10 minutes, or until the edges start to brown. Cool on the baking sheets for 10 minutes. Transfer to a wire rack to cool completely.

SUBSTITUTION TIP: If you don't have instant espresso powder, you can use instant coffee granules instead.

Maple Cookies

Makes 24 cookies

Made with brown sugar and maple syrup, these delightful cookies will have your house smelling like autumn no matter what the season. *Nut-free*

PREP TIME: 10 minutes
COOK TIME: 12 minutes

2½ cups all-purpose flour

2 teaspoons baking powder

½ teaspoon salt

8 tablespoons (1 stick) unsalted butter, room temperature

1 cup light brown sugar

1 large egg, room temperature

1½ teaspoons vanilla extract

½ cup maple syrup

1. **Preheat the oven.** Position a rack in the middle of the oven. Preheat the oven to 375°F. Line two baking sheets with parchment paper or silicone baking mats.

2. **Combine the dry ingredients.** In a small bowl, whisk together the flour, baking powder, and salt.

3. **Cream the butter and sugar.** In a large bowl, using an electric mixer, cream the butter and sugar until light and fluffy, about 2 minutes.

4. **Add the egg, vanilla, and syrup.** Add the egg and beat well. Add the vanilla and maple syrup and mix until just combined.

5. **Add the dry ingredients.** Gradually beat in the flour mixture.

6. **Scoop.** Using a tablespoon, scoop the dough into 1½-inch balls and place them on the baking sheets, leaving about 2 inches between each cookie.

7. **Bake.** Place the baking sheets in the oven on the middle rack and bake for 10 to 12 minutes, or until the cookies are lightly browned on the sides. The centers will look soft. Cool on the baking sheets for 5 minutes. Transfer the cookies to a wire rack to cool completely.

INGREDIENT TIP: I prefer using real maple syrup in these cookies, but if you don't have access to it, you can use the fake stuff (no judgement here!) or 1 to 2 teaspoons of maple extract.

Coconut Macaroons

Makes 14 to 16 cookies

Many coconut macaroons are made with sweetened condensed milk, but these are a more traditional coconut macaroon. Made with whipped egg whites, they're just like ones you might find in a little French bakery. *Dairy-free, Gluten-free*

PREP TIME: 15 minutes
COOK TIME: 20 minutes

4 large egg whites, room temperature

¼ teaspoon salt

½ cup granulated sugar

1 teaspoon vanilla extract

½ teaspoon almond extract

1 (14-ounce) bag shredded sweetened coconut

1. **Preheat the oven.** Preheat the oven to 350°F. Line a baking sheet with parchment paper.

2. **Whip the egg whites.** In a large bowl, using an electric mixer fitted with a whisk attachment and set on low, whip the egg whites, salt, sugar, vanilla, and almond extract until foamy. Increase the speed to medium-high and whip until soft peaks form and the sugar is mostly dissolved, about 2 minutes.

3. **Add the coconut.** Using a rubber spatula, gently fold the coconut into the whipped egg whites.

4. **Scoop.** Scoop the batter in rounded tablespoons and drop each spoonful onto the baking sheet, leaving about 2 inches between each cookie.

5. **Bake.** Bake for about 20 minutes, or until the cookies are golden brown on the top and edges. Cool on the baking sheet for 10 minutes. Transfer the cookies to a wire rack to cool completely.

TROUBLESHOOTING TIP: To make sure that your bowl is clean and that your egg whites whip up properly, wet a paper towel with white vinegar or lemon juice and wipe the inside of the bowl before you begin.

Soft Molasses Cookies

Makes 24 cookies

Every time I visited my grandmother, she had one special kind of cookie in her cupboard for me: crispy gingersnaps. This recipe reinterprets those beloved cookies into a softer and chewier version that's just as irresistible. *Nut-free*

PREP TIME: 10 minutes, plus 1 hour to chill
COOK TIME: 10 minutes

2¼ cups all-purpose flour

1½ teaspoons ground ginger

1½ teaspoons baking soda

1 teaspoon ground cinnamon

½ teaspoon salt

8 tablespoons (1 stick) unsalted butter, room temperature

½ cup granulated sugar

½ cup light brown sugar

1 large egg, room temperature

⅓ cup molasses

1. **Combine the dry ingredients.** In a small bowl, whisk together the flour, ginger, baking soda, cinnamon, and salt.

2. **Cream the butter and sugars.** In a large bowl, using an electric mixer, cream the butter, granulated sugar, and brown sugar until light and fluffy, about 2 minutes.

3. **Add the egg and molasses.** Add the egg, mixing well until incorporated. Add the molasses and mix until just combined. Scrape down the bowl as needed.

4. **Add the dry ingredients.** Gradually beat in the flour mixture.

5. **Refrigerate the dough.** Refrigerate the dough for at least 1 hour, until firm.

6. **Preheat the oven.** Preheat the oven to 375°F. Line two baking sheets with parchment paper or silicone baking mats.

7. **Scoop.** Using a tablespoon, scoop the dough into 1½-inch balls and place them on the baking sheets, leaving about 2 inches between each cookie.

8. **Bake.** Bake for 10 to 12 minutes, or until lightly browned on the sides. The centers will look soft. Cool on the baking sheets for 5 minutes. Transfer the cookies to a wire rack to cool completely.

INGREDIENT TIP: For easy cleanup, spray your measuring cup with nonstick cooking spray before measuring the molasses.

Soft Peanut Butter Cookies

Makes 24 cookies

The key to really satisfyingly soft peanut butter cookies is to make sure to not overbake them so the sweet peanut buttery flavor and pillowy texture can take center stage.

PREP TIME: **15 minutes**
COOK TIME: **12 minutes**

8 tablespoons (1 stick) unsalted butter, room temperature

¼ cup granulated sugar, plus more for topping

¾ cup light brown sugar

1 large egg, room temperature

1 cup smooth peanut butter

1 teaspoon vanilla extract

½ teaspoon salt

½ teaspoon baking soda

1½ cups all-purpose flour

1. **Preheat the oven.** Preheat the oven to 375°F. Line two baking sheets with parchment paper or silicone baking mats.

2. **Cream the butter and sugar.** In a large bowl, using an electric mixer, cream the butter, granulated sugar, and brown sugar until light and fluffy, about 2 minutes.

3. **Add the remaining wet ingredients.** Mix in the egg. Add the peanut butter and vanilla and mix until smooth and creamy.

4. **Add the dry ingredients.** Add the salt, baking soda, and flour and mix until well combined.

5. **Scoop.** Put the sugar for the topping in a shallow bowl. Using a tablespoon, scoop the dough into 1-inch balls, then roll each dough ball in the sugar. Place the dough balls on the baking sheets, leaving about 2 inches between each cookie. Using a fork, make a crisscross pattern on the top of each cookie by pressing down with the fork in one direction, then rotating the fork 90 degrees and pressing down again.

6. **Bake.** Bake the cookies for 10 to 12 minutes, or until the tops are set. Cool on the baking sheets for 5 minutes. Transfer the cookies to a wire rack to cool completely.

PREPARATION TIP: To make peanut butter blossoms, do not make the crisscross pattern in step 5; instead leave the dough in balls and bake. When the cookies come out of the oven, press a chocolate kiss firmly into the center of each one.

Oatmeal Cookies

Makes 36 cookies

To achieve the best texture, I recommend refrigerating this dough overnight. But if your oatmeal cookie craving needs immediate attention, feel free to bake the cookies right away. *Nut-free*

PREP TIME: 15 minutes, plus overnight to chill (optional)
COOK TIME: 12 minutes

2 cups all-purpose flour

1 teaspoon baking soda

1 teaspoon salt

1 teaspoon ground cinnamon

1 cup (2 sticks) unsalted butter, melted and slightly cooled

1 cup light brown sugar

½ cup granulated sugar

2 large eggs, room temperature

1 teaspoon vanilla extract

2 cups old-fashioned oats

1½ cups raisins or chocolate chips (optional)

1. **Preheat the oven.** Position a rack in the middle of the oven. Preheat the oven to 350°F. Line two baking sheets with parchment paper or silicone baking mats.

2. **Combine the dry ingredients.** In a medium bowl, whisk together the flour, baking soda, salt, and cinnamon.

3. **Combine the wet ingredients.** In a large bowl, stir together the melted butter, brown sugar, and granulated sugar. Mix in the eggs and vanilla.

4. **Add the dry ingredients.** Add the flour mixture to the butter and sugar and stir until just combined.

5. **Stir in the oats.** With a rubber spatula, stir in the oats and the raisins or chocolate chips, if using.

6. **Scoop.** Using a tablespoon, scoop the dough into 1½-inch balls and place them on the baking sheets, leaving about 2 inches between each cookie. Cover and refrigerate overnight.

7. **Bake.** Place the baking sheets in the oven on the middle rack and bake for 10 to 12 minutes, or until the cookies are lightly browned on the sides. The centers will look soft. Cool on the baking sheets for 5 minutes. Transfer the cookies to a wire rack to cool completely.

SUBSTITUTION TIP: Instead of semisweet chocolate chips, try using white chocolate chips, or swap out the raisins for dried cranberries.

Perfect Chocolate Chip Cookies

Makes 48 cookies

I need to give my sister, who makes perfect chocolate chip cookies, some credit for this recipe. It really is perfect. *Nut-free*

PREP TIME: **10 minutes**
COOK TIME: **12 minutes**

3 cups all-purpose flour

1 teaspoon baking soda

¼ teaspoon baking powder

1 teaspoon salt

1 cup (2 sticks) unsalted butter, room temperature

½ cup granulated sugar

1 cup light brown sugar

2 large eggs, room temperature

1 teaspoon vanilla extract

2 cups semisweet chocolate chips

1. **Preheat the oven.** Position a rack in the middle of the oven. Preheat the oven to 375°F. Line two baking sheets with parchment paper or silicone baking mats.

2. **Combine the dry ingredients.** In a small bowl, whisk together the flour, baking soda, baking powder, and salt.

3. **Cream the butter and sugars.** In a large bowl, using an electric mixer, cream the butter, granulated sugar, and brown sugar until light and fluffy, about 2 minutes.

4. **Add the eggs and vanilla.** Add the eggs, one at a time, mixing well after each addition. Add the vanilla and mix until just combined.

5. **Add the dry ingredients.** Gradually beat in the flour mixture. Using a rubber spatula, stir in the chocolate chips.

6. **Scoop.** Using a tablespoon, scoop the dough into 1½-inch balls and place them on the baking sheets, leaving about 2 inches between each cookie.

7. **Bake.** Place the baking sheet in the oven on the middle rack and bake for 10 to 12 minutes, or until the cookies are lightly browned on the sides. The centers will look soft. Cool on the baking sheets for 5 minutes. Transfer the cookies to a wire rack to cool completely.

TROUBLESHOOTING TIP: To soften your butter quickly, microwave it for 30 seconds at 20 percent power. Then flip the butter and repeat until just softened.

Pistachio Cookies

Makes 18 cookies

Many pistachio cookie recipes rely on artificial pudding mix to achieve their nutty taste. This recipe skips the mix, using almond extract and chopped pistachios instead for a more nuanced flavor.

PREP TIME: **10 minutes**
COOK TIME: **12 minutes**

1½ cups all-purpose flour

½ teaspoon baking soda

½ teaspoon salt

8 tablespoons (1 stick) unsalted butter, room temperature

½ cup granulated sugar

½ cup light brown sugar

1 large egg, room temperature

1 teaspoon vanilla extract

1 teaspoon almond extract

½ cup chopped pistachios

½ cup white chocolate chips

1. **Preheat the oven.** Preheat the oven to 375°F. Line two baking sheets with parchment paper or silicone baking mats.

2. **Combine the dry ingredients.** In a small bowl, whisk together the flour, baking soda, and salt.

3. **Cream the butter and sugars.** In a large bowl, using an electric mixer, cream the butter, granulated sugar, and brown sugar until light and fluffy, about 2 minutes.

4. **Add the egg and extracts.** Mix in the egg. Add the vanilla and almond extracts and mix until just combined. Scrape down the bowl as needed.

5. **Add the dry ingredients.** Add the flour mixture and mix until just combined. Using a rubber spatula, stir in the pistachios and chocolate chips.

6. **Scoop.** Using a tablespoon, scoop the dough into 1½-inch balls and drop them onto the baking sheets, leaving about 2 inches between each cookie.

7. **Bake.** Bake for 10 to 12 minutes, or until the cookies are lightly browned on the sides. The centers will look soft. Cool on the baking sheet for 5 minutes. Transfer the cookies to a wire rack to cool completely.

SUBSTITUTION TIP: Feel free to substitute chopped almonds for the pistachios.

Pumpkin and White Chocolate Chip Cookies

Makes 32 cookies

Featuring cloves, nutmeg, ginger, and pumpkin, these cookies are guaranteed winners. *Nut-free*

PREP TIME: 15 minutes, plus 1 hour to chill
COOK TIME: 12 minutes

3 cups all-purpose flour

2 teaspoons baking powder

1 teaspoon baking soda

1 teaspoon salt

2 teaspoons ground cinnamon

1 teaspoon ground ginger

½ teaspoon ground cloves

¼ teaspoon ground nutmeg

1 cup (2 sticks) unsalted butter, melted and slightly cooled

⅔ cup pumpkin purée

1 cup light brown sugar

½ cup granulated sugar

1 tablespoon vanilla extract

2 large eggs, room temperature

2 cups white chocolate chips

1. **Combine the dry ingredients.** In a medium bowl, whisk together the flour, baking powder, baking soda, salt, cinnamon, ginger, cloves, and nutmeg.

2. **Combine the wet ingredients.** In a large bowl, combine the butter, pumpkin purée, brown sugar, granulated sugar, vanilla, and eggs, whisking until thoroughly combined.

3. **Add the dry ingredients.** Add the flour mixture to the pumpkin mixture and stir until incorporated. Stir in the chocolate chips.

4. **Refrigerate the dough.** Turn the dough out onto a sheet of plastic wrap and wrap it tightly. Refrigerate for 1 hour, or until firm.

5. **Preheat the oven.** About 15 minutes before baking, preheat the oven to 350°F. Line two baking sheets with parchment paper or silicone baking mats.

6. **Scoop.** Using a tablespoon, scoop the dough into 1½-inch balls and drop them on the baking sheets, leaving about 2 inches between each cookie.

7. **Bake.** Bake for 10 to 12 minutes, or until the cookies are lightly browned on the sides. The centers will look soft. Cool on the baking sheets for 5 minutes. Transfer the cookies to a wire rack to cool completely.

INGREDIENT TIP: For the best results, be sure to use pumpkin purée, not pumpkin pie mix.

Chocolate Brownie Cookies

Makes 24 cookies

These treats take all the things you love about brownies—
fudgy middles, chewy edges, and amazing chocolate
flavor—and put them in cookie form. *Nut-free*

PREP TIME: **15 minutes**
COOK TIME: **12 minutes**

1¾ cups all-purpose flour

½ cup unsweetened
    cocoa powder

½ teaspoon salt

¼ teaspoon baking soda

11 tablespoons
    unsalted butter,
    room temperature

1½ cups light brown sugar

2 large eggs, room
    temperature

1 teaspoon vanilla extract

2 cups semisweet
    chocolate chips

1. **Preheat the oven.** Position a rack in the middle of the oven. Preheat the oven to 375°F. Line two baking sheets with parchment paper or silicone baking mats.

2. **Combine the dry ingredients.** In a small bowl, whisk together the flour, cocoa powder, salt, and baking soda.

3. **Cream the butter and sugar.** In a large bowl, using an electric mixer, cream the butter and sugar until light and fluffy, about 2 minutes.

4. **Add the eggs and vanilla.** Add the eggs, one at a time, mixing well after each addition. Scrape down the bowl as needed. Mix in the vanilla.

5. **Add the dry ingredients.** Turn the electric mixer to low and gradually beat in the flour mixture until just combined. Using a rubber spatula, stir in the chocolate chips.

6. **Scoop.** Using a tablespoon, scoop the dough into 1½-inch balls and drop them onto the baking sheets, leaving about 2 inches between each cookie.

7. **Bake.** Place the baking sheets in the oven on the middle rack and bake for 10 to 12 minutes, or until the cookies are lightly browned on the sides. The centers will look soft. Cool on the baking sheets for 5 minutes. Transfer the cookies to a wire rack to cool completely.

TROUBLESHOOTING TIP: If your cookies are spreading too much as they bake, try chilling the dough for 30 minutes to 1 hour before starting the next batch.

Spiced Hot Chocolate Cookies

Makes 32 cookies

Loaded with richness from the chocolate, warmth from the cinnamon, and zing from the chili powder, these cookies deliver decadent chocolate flavor and a fun pop of heat. *Nut-free*

PREP TIME: 10 minutes
COOK TIME: 12 minutes

2¼ cups all-purpose flour

½ cup unsweetened cocoa powder

2 teaspoons ground cinnamon

1 teaspoon chili powder

1 teaspoon baking soda

½ teaspoon salt

1 cup (2 sticks) unsalted butter, room temperature

1 cup light brown sugar

¾ cup granulated sugar

2 large eggs, room temperature

1 teaspoon vanilla extract

2 cups semisweet chocolate chips

1. **Preheat the oven.** Preheat the oven to 375°F. Line two baking sheets with parchment paper or silicone baking mats.

2. **Combine the dry ingredients.** In a small bowl, whisk together the flour, cocoa powder, cinnamon, chili powder, baking soda, and salt.

3. **Cream the butter and sugars.** In a large bowl, using an electric mixer, cream the butter, brown sugar, and granulated sugar until light and fluffy, about 2 minutes.

4. **Add the eggs and vanilla.** Add the eggs, one at a time, mixing well after each addition. Mix in the vanilla.

5. **Add the dry ingredients.** Gradually beat in the flour mixture. Using a rubber spatula, stir in the chocolate chips.

6. **Scoop.** Using a tablespoon, scoop the dough into 1½-inch balls and place them on the baking sheets, leaving about 2 inches between each cookie.

7. **Bake.** Bake for 10 to 12 minutes, or until the cookies are lightly browned on the sides. The centers will look soft. Cool on a baking sheet for 5 minutes. Transfer the cookies to a wire rack to cool completely.

PREPARATION TIP: Remove the cookies from the oven after 8 minutes. Top each with a few mini marshmallows, then pop them back into the oven until the marshmallows are just toasted, about 2 minutes.

Monster Cookies

Makes 36 cookies

If I ever renamed these cookies, I'd call them the "Everything Cookie" because they are everything I love in a cookie.

PREP TIME: 15 minutes
COOK TIME: 12 minutes

1 cup all-purpose flour

1 cup old-fashioned oats

½ teaspoon baking soda

½ teaspoon salt

8 tablespoons (1 stick) unsalted butter, room temperature

½ cup light brown sugar

½ cup granulated sugar

1 large egg, room temperature

½ teaspoon vanilla extract

½ cup smooth peanut butter

1 cup semisweet chocolate chips

1 cup chocolate-coated candies

1. **Preheat the oven.** Position a rack in the middle of the oven. Preheat the oven to 350°F. Line two baking sheets with parchment paper or silicone baking mats.

2. **Combine the dry ingredients.** In a medium bowl, whisk together the flour, oats, baking soda, and salt.

3. **Cream the butter and sugar.** In a large bowl, using an electric mixer, cream the butter, brown sugar, and granulated sugar until light and fluffy, about 2 minutes.

4. **Add the remaining wet ingredients.** Mix in the egg. Scrape down the bowl as needed. Add the vanilla and mix well. Mix in the peanut butter.

5. **Add the dry ingredients.** Add the dry ingredients to the wet ingredients and mix just until no flour streaks remain. Using a rubber spatula, stir in the chocolate chips and candies.

6. **Scoop.** Using a tablespoon, scoop the dough into 1½-inch balls and place them on the baking sheets, leaving about 2 inches between each cookie.

7. **Bake.** Place the baking sheets in the oven on the middle rack and bake for 10 to 12 minutes, or until the cookies are lightly browned on the sides. The centers will look soft. Cool on the baking sheets for 5 minutes. Transfer the cookies to a wire rack to cool completely.

SUBSTITUTION TIP: For a little crunch, try using chunky peanut butter instead of smooth.

Red Velvet Chocolate Chip Cookies

Makes 18 cookies

These are the ideal cookies to make around Christmas or
for Valentine's Day, and, true to their namesake, they have
a hint of cocoa and a bit of tang from the buttermilk.

PREP TIME: **15 minutes**
COOK TIME: **10 minutes**

2 cups all-purpose flour

¼ cup unsweetened
cocoa powder

1 teaspoon baking soda

½ teaspoon baking
powder

½ teaspoon salt

8 tablespoons (1 stick)
unsalted butter,
room temperature

¾ cup light brown sugar

¼ cup granulated sugar

1 large egg, room
temperature

1½ tablespoons
buttermilk or
regular milk

1½ teaspoons vanilla
extract

1 tablespoon red food
coloring

1 cup white chocolate
chips

1. **Preheat the oven**. Preheat the oven to 350°F. Line
two baking sheets with parchment paper or silicone
baking mats.

2. **Combine the dry ingredients**. In a small bowl,
whisk together the flour, cocoa powder, baking soda,
baking powder, and salt.

3. **Cream the butter and sugars.** In a large bowl, using
an electric mixer, cream the butter, brown sugar, and
granulated sugar until light and fluffy, about 2 minutes.

4. **Add the remaining wet ingredients.** Mix the egg,
buttermilk, and vanilla into the butter mixture until
smooth. Mix in the food coloring until the batter is a
uniform color.

5. **Add the dry ingredients.** Turn the electric mixer to
low and gradually beat in the flour mixture until just combined. Using a rubber spatula, stir in the chocolate chips.

6. **Scoop.** Using a tablespoon, scoop the dough into
1½-inch balls and drop them on the baking sheets,
leaving about 2 inches between each cookie. Slightly
flatten each ball of dough.

7. **Bake.** Bake for about 10 minutes, or until the edges
of the cookies are lightly browned. Cool on the baking
sheets for 5 minutes. Transfer the cookies to a wire rack
to cool completely.

SUBSTITUTION TIP: These are great made with semisweet chocolate chips instead or dipped in melted white
chocolate after they've cooled.

Iced Lime Meltaways

Makes 24 cookies

Combining classic Key lime–style brightness with buttery cookie dough, these treats practically melt in your mouth when you bite into them. *Nut-free*

PREP TIME: 10 minutes, plus 2 hours to chill

COOK TIME: 10 minutes

FOR THE COOKIES

1¼ cups all-purpose flour

12 tablespoons (1½ sticks) unsalted butter, room temperature

½ cup cornstarch

⅓ cup powdered sugar

1 teaspoon vanilla extract

1 tablespoon freshly squeezed lime juice

1 teaspoon grated lime zest

FOR THE ICING

¾ cup powdered sugar

2 tablespoons freshly squeezed lime juice

1 tablespoon grated lime zest (optional)

TO MAKE THE COOKIES

1. Make the cookie dough. In a large bowl, combine all the cookie ingredients. Using an electric mixer set on low, mix the ingredients until well combined, about 2 minutes. Scrape down the bowl as needed.

2. Shape and refrigerate the dough. Turn the dough out onto a 12-inch piece of plastic wrap and shape into a log about 1 inch thick and 9 inches long. Tightly wrap the dough and refrigerate for 1 to 2 hours, or until firm.

3. Preheat the oven. About 15 minutes before baking, preheat the oven to 350°F. Line two baking sheets with parchment paper or silicone baking mats.

4. Bake. Unwrap the dough and use a sharp knife to cut the log into ¼-inch slices. Place the slices on the baking sheets, leaving about 2 inches between each cookie. Bake for 8 to 10 minutes or until the cookies have set (they will not brown). Cool on the baking sheets for 5 minutes. Transfer the cookies to a wire rack to cool completely.

TO MAKE THE ICING

Make the icing and ice the cookies. In a small bowl, whisk together all the icing ingredients. Spread the icing over the cooled cookies.

SUBSTITUTION TIP: These cookies would be great with any type of citrus. Try using lemon or orange for a different twist.

Glazed Orange Ricotta Cookies

Makes 24 cookies

When citrus is in season, it's the perfect time to make these delicate, light cookies. The ricotta cheese makes them especially soft and moist. *Nut-free*

PREP TIME: 10 minutes
COOK TIME: 10 minutes

FOR THE COOKIES

2½ cups all-purpose flour

½ teaspoon baking soda

½ teaspoon baking powder

½ teaspoon salt

8 tablespoons (1 stick) unsalted butter, room temperature

1 cup granulated sugar

1 large egg, room temperature

1 cup (8 ounces) ricotta cheese, room temperature

1 teaspoon vanilla extract

2½ tablespoons orange juice

1 tablespoon grated orange zest

FOR THE GLAZE

¾ cup powdered sugar

2 tablespoons orange juice

TO MAKE THE COOKIES

1. **Preheat the oven.** Preheat the oven to 350°F. Line two baking sheets with parchment paper or silicone baking mats.

2. **Combine the dry ingredients.** In a small bowl, whisk together the flour, baking soda, baking powder, and salt.

3. **Cream the butter and sugar.** In a large bowl, using an electric mixer, cream the butter and sugar until light and fluffy, about 2 minutes. Scrape down the bowl as needed.

4. **Add the remaining wet ingredients.** Mix in the egg. Add the ricotta, vanilla, orange juice, and orange zest and mix until combined.

5. **Add the dry ingredients.** Gradually beat in the flour mixture.

6. **Scoop.** Using a tablespoon, scoop the dough into 1½-inch balls and place them on the baking sheets, leaving about 2 inches between each cookie.

7. **Bake.** Place the baking sheets in the oven on the middle rack and bake for 8 to 10 minutes or until the cookies are lightly browned on the sides. Cool on the baking sheets for 5 minutes. Transfer the cookies to a wire rack to cool completely.

TO MAKE THE GLAZE

Make the glaze and glaze the cookies. In a small bowl, whisk together the glaze ingredients. Spread the glaze over the cooled cookies.

Carrot Cake and Oatmeal Cookie Sandwiches

Makes 24 cookies (12 sandwiches)

Combining the best of both worlds, this recipe marries carrot cake with oatmeal cream pies.

PREP TIME: **20 minutes**
COOK TIME: **20 minutes**

FOR THE COOKIES

1 cup shredded carrots

1 tablespoon light brown sugar

1½ cups all-purpose flour

½ teaspoon salt

½ teaspoon baking powder

¼ teaspoon ground nutmeg

2 teaspoons ground cinnamon

⅛ teaspoon ground cloves

1 cup (2 sticks) unsalted butter, room temperature

1 cup light brown sugar

1 cup granulated sugar

2 large eggs, room temperature

3 cups old-fashioned oats

1 cup shredded sweetened coconut

1 cup toasted chopped walnuts

1 cup raisins

TO MAKE THE COOKIES

1. **Preheat the oven.** Preheat the oven to 350°F. Line two baking sheets with parchment paper or silicone baking mats.

2. **Drain the carrots.** Place the carrots in a colander set over a bowl. Sprinkle with the brown sugar. Let the carrots drain while you prepare the cookie dough.

3. **Combine the dry ingredients.** In a small bowl, whisk together the flour, salt, baking powder, nutmeg, cinnamon, and cloves.

4. **Cream the butter and sugars.** In a large bowl, using an electric mixer, cream the butter and brown and granulated sugars until light and fluffy, about 2 minutes.

5. **Add the eggs and carrots.** Add the eggs, one at a time, mixing well after each addition. Scrape down the bowl as needed. Mix in the carrots.

6. **Add the dry ingredients.** Gradually beat in the flour mixture. Using a rubber spatula, stir in the oats, coconut, walnuts, and raisins.

7. **Scoop.** Using a cookie scoop or two spoons, scoop the dough into 24 (2-inch) balls and place them on the baking sheets, leaving about 2 inches between each cookie.

8. **Bake.** Bake for 18 to 20 minutes, or until the edges turn golden brown. Cool for 5 minutes. Transfer the cookies to a wire rack to cool completely.

FOR THE FROSTING

8 ounces cream cheese, room temperature

8 tablespoons (1 stick) unsalted butter, room temperature

3 cups powdered sugar

Pinch salt

2 teaspoons vanilla extract

TO MAKE THE FROSTING

1. **Make the frosting.** In a large bowl, combine all the frosting ingredients. Using an electric mixer set on low speed, mix the ingredients together. When the powdered sugar has been incorporated, gradually increase the speed to medium. Mix until smooth.

2. **Frost the cookies.** When the cookies have completely cooled, frost the top of each cookie. Or, for cookie sandwiches, frost the bottom of one cookie and press the bottom of a second cookie into the frosting.

Fudgy Chocolate Brownies PAGE 47

4

Basically Brownies
and Bars

Frosted Sugar Cookie Bars 44

Cookies and Cream Bars 45

Butterscotch Blondies 46

Fudgy Chocolate Brownies 47

Pumpkin Bars 48

Maple-Peach Bars 49

Banoffee Bars 50

Oatmeal Chocolate Chip
Cookie Bars 51

S'mores Bars 52

Lemon Bars 53

Pecan Pie Bars 54

Apple Pie Bars 55

Raspberry Jam Bars 56

Raspberry Cheesecake Brownies 57

Frosted Sugar Cookie Bars

Makes 20 to 24 bars

These soft, chewy sugar cookie bars—loaded with sprinkles and topped with creamy vanilla buttercream—are sure to put a smile on your face. *Nut-free*

PREP TIME: 15 minutes
COOK TIME: 30 minutes

2¼ cups all-purpose flour

¼ teaspoon salt

½ teaspoon baking soda

1 teaspoon cornstarch

1 cup (2 sticks) unsalted butter, room temperature

1 cup granulated sugar

2 large eggs, room temperature

1½ teaspoons vanilla extract

½ cup sprinkles, plus more for topping

Vanilla Buttercream (page 176)

1. **Preheat the oven.** Preheat the oven to 350°F. Lightly coat a 9-by-13-inch baking pan with cooking spray or line with parchment paper.

2. **Combine the dry ingredients.** In a small bowl, whisk together the flour, salt, baking soda, and cornstarch.

3. **Combine the wet ingredients.** In a large bowl, using an electric mixer, cream the butter and sugar until light and fluffy, about 2 minutes. Add the eggs, one at a time, mixing well after each addition. Scrape down the bowl as needed. Mix in the vanilla.

4. **Add the dry ingredients.** Add the dry ingredients to the wet ingredients and stir until just combined.

5. **Fold in the sprinkles.** Fold in the sprinkles until just combined. Spread the batter into the prepared pan.

6. **Bake.** Bake for about 30 minutes, or until the bars are lightly browned and a toothpick inserted into the center comes out clean. Set the pan on a wire rack and cool completely. When the bars are completely cool, spread the buttercream over the top in an even layer. Top with more sprinkles, if desired, and cut into bars.

INGREDIENT TIP: In baking, cornstarch can help soften the proteins in the flour, making a softer bar.

Cookies and Cream Bars

Makes 16 bars

You can't help but love a dessert that can be made in one bowl and contains everyone's favorite chocolate sandwich cookie. *Nut-free*

PREP TIME: 10 minutes
COOK TIME: 30 minutes

1 cup (2 sticks)
  unsalted butter,
  room temperature

1 cup (8 ounces)
  cream cheese,
  room temperature

1½ cups granulated sugar

1 large egg, room
  temperature

2 teaspoons vanilla
  extract

2½ cups all-purpose flour

½ teaspoon baking
  powder

½ teaspoon salt

1 cup crushed chocolate
  sandwich cookies

1 cup white
  chocolate chips

1. **Preheat the oven.** Preheat the oven to 350°F. Lightly coat a 9-by-13-inch baking pan with cooking spray or line with parchment paper.

2. **Make the batter.** In a medium bowl, using an electric mixer set on medium, cream the butter, cream cheese, and sugar, 2 to 3 minutes. Scrape down the bowl as needed. Add the egg and vanilla, beating until combined. Add the flour, baking powder, and salt and mix until incorporated. Using a rubber spatula, stir in the crushed cookies and chocolate chips.

3. **Bake.** Using a rubber spatula, spread the batter in the pan in an even layer. Bake for 25 to 30 minutes, or until the center is set. Set the pan on a wire rack and cool completely before cutting into bars.

TROUBLESHOOTING TIP: To make spreading the batter in the pan easier, spray a piece of plastic wrap with cooking spray and use it to press down the batter evenly.

Butterscotch Blondies

Makes 16 bars

Even though these bars may not appear fully done when
the timer goes off, take them out right after 30 minutes.
They will firm up once they've cooled. *Nut-free*

PREP TIME: **10 minutes**
COOK TIME: **30 minutes**

2 cups all-purpose flour

1 teaspoon salt

12 tablespoons (1½ sticks)
   unsalted butter,
   room temperature

1½ cups light brown sugar

3 large eggs, room
   temperature

1 tablespoon vanilla
   extract

2 cups butterscotch chips

1. **Preheat the oven.** Preheat the oven to 325°F. Lightly
coat a 9-by-13-inch baking pan with cooking spray or
line with parchment paper.

2. **Combine the dry ingredients**. In a small bowl,
whisk together the flour and salt.

3. **Combine the wet ingredients.** In a large bowl, using
an electric mixer, cream the butter and sugar until light
and fluffy, about 2 minutes. Add the eggs, one at a time,
mixing well after each addition. Mix in the vanilla.

4. **Add the dry ingredients**. Using a rubber spatula,
stir in the flour mixture until just combined. Fold in the
butterscotch chips.

5. **Bake.** Spread the batter in the pan in an even layer
and bake for 30 minutes, or until the edges are golden
brown. The center of the bars will still jiggle. Set the
pan on a wire rack and cool completely before cutting
into bars.

SUBSTITUTION TIP: If you don't have butterscotch
chips on hand, nearly any type of chips will work! Just
keep the amount to 2 cups.

Fudgy Chocolate Brownies

Makes 12 brownies

These wonderfully chocolatey brownies offer the crackly top
one looks for in a gold medal–worthy brownie recipe.

PREP TIME: 10 minutes
COOK TIME: 25 minutes

8 tablespoons (1 stick)
  unsalted butter,
  melted and slightly
  cooled

1¼ cups granulated sugar

2 large eggs, room
  temperature

1 teaspoon vanilla extract

¾ cup unsweetened
  cocoa powder

⅓ cup all-purpose flour

¼ teaspoon salt

¼ teaspoon baking
  powder

½ cup semisweet
  chocolate chips

½ cup walnuts or pecans,
  chopped and toasted
  (optional)

1. **Preheat the oven.** Preheat the oven to 350°F. Butter
and flour an 8-by-8-inch baking pan.

2. **Combine the wet ingredients.** Whisk together the
butter, sugar, eggs, and vanilla.

3. **Add the dry ingredients.** Using a rubber spatula,
stir in the cocoa powder, flour, salt, and baking powder.
Fold in the chocolate chips and nuts, if using.

4. **Bake.** Spread the batter in the pan in an even layer.
Bake for 25 minutes, or until the top is set and a toothpick inserted into the center comes out with moist
crumbs. Set the pan on a wire rack and cool completely
before cutting into bars.

SUBSTITUTION TIP: Make these brownies minty by
adding ½ teaspoon of peppermint extract and ½ cup of
mint-flavored chocolate chips.

Pumpkin Bars

Makes 30 bars

These moist bars are so full of warm spices, like cinnamon
and nutmeg, that all they need is a nice layer of Cream
Cheese Frosting (page 175) on top. *Nut-free*

PREP TIME: 10 minutes
COOK TIME: 30 minutes

2 cups all-purpose flour

1 teaspoon baking
powder

½ teaspoon baking soda

2 teaspoons ground
cinnamon

½ teaspoon ground
ginger

¼ teaspoon ground
nutmeg

¼ teaspoon ground
cloves

1 teaspoon salt

3 large eggs, room
temperature

1½ cups granulated sugar

1 cup vegetable oil

1 (29-ounce) can pumpkin
purée

1. **Preheat the oven.** Preheat the oven to 350°F. Lightly
coat a rimmed baking sheet with cooking spray.

2. **Combine the dry ingredients.** In a small bowl, combine the flour, baking powder, baking soda, cinnamon,
ginger, nutmeg, cloves, and salt.

3. **Combine the wet ingredients.** In a large bowl,
whisk together the eggs, sugar, oil, and pumpkin purée
until well combined.

4. **Add the dry ingredients.** Stir the dry ingredients
into the pumpkin mixture until thoroughly combined.

5. **Bake.** Spread the batter on the baking sheet in an
even layer. Bake for 25 to 30 minutes, or until a toothpick inserted into the center comes out clean. Set the
pan on a wire rack and cool completely before cutting
into bars.

PREPARATION TIP: For thicker bars, bake these in a
9-by-13-inch pan for 30 to 35 minutes.

Maple-Peach Bars

Makes 20 bars

Peaches are one of my favorite summer fruits and this bar is a perfect way to enjoy ripe, juicy peaches when they're in season. *Nut-free*

PREP TIME: 20 minutes
COOK TIME: 30 minutes

2 cups all-purpose flour

¾ teaspoon salt

½ teaspoon ground cinnamon

¼ teaspoon baking soda

1⅓ cups light brown sugar

8 tablespoons (1 stick) unsalted butter, melted and slightly cooled

½ cup maple syrup

2 teaspoons vanilla extract

2 large eggs, room temperature

3 cups peeled, chopped peaches (about 3 medium peaches)

½ cup peach preserves

1. **Preheat the oven.** Preheat the oven to 350°F. Lightly coat a 9-by-13-inch baking pan with cooking spray or line with parchment paper.

2. **Combine the dry ingredients.** In a small bowl, combine the flour, salt, cinnamon, and baking soda.

3. **Combine the wet ingredients.** In a large bowl, whisk together the sugar, butter, maple syrup, vanilla, and eggs until smooth.

4. **Add the dry ingredients.** Add the dry ingredients to the wet ingredients and stir until just combined.

5. **Fold in the peaches.** Using a rubber spatula, gently fold in the peaches. Pour the batter into the prepared pan.

6. **Add the preserves.** Spoon several dollops of preserves over the batter, then use a knife to create swirls of jam in the batter.

7. **Bake.** Bake for 25 to 30 minutes, or until golden brown and a toothpick inserted into the center comes out clean. Set the pan on a wire rack and cool completely before cutting into bars.

SUBSTITUTION TIP: For a boost, add a maple glaze. Make the Powdered Sugar Glaze (page 170) and add ¼ cup of maple syrup. Spread the glaze over these bars once they've completely cooled.

Banoffee Bars

Makes 20 bars

Banoffee is a delicious combination of bananas and caramel that was invented in England at a restaurant called The Hungry Monk. Part cake and part banana bread, these bars are 100 percent scrumptious. *Nut-free*

PREP TIME: 10 minutes
COOK TIME: 30 minutes

½ cup light brown sugar

½ cup granulated sugar

⅓ cup vegetable oil

2 large eggs, room temperature

½ teaspoon vanilla extract

1 cup mashed bananas (about 2 medium bananas)

1 cup all-purpose flour

1 teaspoon baking soda

½ teaspoon baking powder

½ teaspoon salt

¼ teaspoon ground cinnamon

½ cup caramel sauce, homemade or store-bought

1. **Preheat the oven.** Preheat the oven to 350°F. Lightly coat a 9-by-13-inch baking pan with cooking spray or line with parchment paper.

2. **Combine the wet ingredients.** In a large bowl, whisk together the brown sugar, granulated sugar, oil, eggs, vanilla, and bananas.

3. **Add the dry ingredients.** Stir in the flour, baking soda, baking powder, salt, and cinnamon until just combined.

4. **Add the caramel sauce.** Stir in the caramel sauce and spoon the batter into the pan.

5. **Bake.** Bake for 25 to 30 minutes, or until a toothpick inserted into the center comes out clean. Set the pan on a wire rack and cool completely before cutting into bars.

PREPARATION TIP: Although delicious on their own, these bars are even more delectable with Caramel Icing (page 173) spread over the cooled bars before cutting.

Oatmeal Chocolate Chip Cookie Bars

Makes 16 bars

These delectable bars are everything you love about oatmeal cookies but even easier to make. *Nut-free*

PREP TIME: 10 minutes
COOK TIME: 25 minutes

1½ cups all-purpose flour

2 cups old-fashioned oats

1 teaspoon baking powder

½ teaspoon salt

1 cup (2 sticks) unsalted butter, melted and slightly cooled

1 cup light brown sugar

1 cup granulated sugar

2 large eggs, room temperature

1 teaspoon vanilla extract

2 cups semisweet chocolate chips

1. **Preheat the oven.** Preheat the oven to 375°F. Lightly coat a 9-by-13-inch baking pan with cooking spray or line with parchment paper.

2. **Combine the dry ingredients.** In a small bowl, combine the flour, oats, baking powder, and salt.

3. **Combine the wet ingredients.** In a large bowl, whisk together the butter, brown sugar, granulated sugar, eggs, and vanilla.

4. **Add the dry ingredients.** Using a rubber spatula, stir in the flour mixture until just combined. Fold in the chocolate chips.

5. **Bake.** Spread the batter in the pan in an even layer. Bake for 20 to 25 minutes, or until the edges are golden brown. The center of the bars will still jiggle. Set the pan on a wire rack until the center is set and cooled completely before cutting the bars.

SUBSTITUTION TIP: Have fun with these bars and use what you have on hand, like dark chocolate chips, raisins, or toasted and coarsely chopped nuts.

S'mores Bars

Makes 16 bars

These gooey bars are everything you love about
s'mores—no campfire necessary. *Nut-free*

PREP TIME: 15 minutes
COOK TIME: 30 minutes

2 cups all-purpose flour

2 cups graham cracker
   crumbs

1 teaspoon salt

12 tablespoons (1½ sticks)
   unsalted butter,
   room temperature

½ cup granulated sugar

1 cup light brown sugar

3 large eggs, room
   temperature

2 teaspoons vanilla
   extract

2 cups milk chocolate
   chips

2 cups miniature
   marshmallows

1. **Preheat the oven.** Preheat the oven to 325°F. Lightly coat a 9-by-13-inch baking pan with cooking spray or line with parchment paper.

2. **Combine the dry ingredients.** In a large bowl, whisk together the flour, graham cracker crumbs, and salt.

3. **Combine the wet ingredients.** In a separate large bowl, using an electric mixer, cream the butter, granulated sugar, and brown sugar until light and fluffy, about 2 minutes. Add the eggs, one at a time, beating well after each addition. Scrape down the bowl as needed. Mix in the vanilla.

4. **Add the dry ingredients.** Stir in the flour mixture until just combined. Spread the batter in the pan. Using a piece of greased plastic wrap, press the batter down into the pan in a compact, even layer.

5. **Bake.** Bake for 30 minutes, or until the top is set and golden brown and a toothpick inserted into the center comes out clean.

6. **Add the chocolate chips and marshmallows.** Remove the pan from the oven and sprinkle the chocolate chips and marshmallows over the top.

7. **Broil.** Turn the oven to broil and return the bars to the oven for 1 to 2 minutes, or until the marshmallows are lightly toasted. Set the pan on a wire rack and cool completely before cutting into bars.

INGREDIENT TIP: To make graham cracker crumbs, pulse crackers in a food processor until finely ground.

Lemon Bars

Makes 20 bars

In this one-bowl recipe, a tart and luscious layer of lemon curd sits on a buttery, shortbread crust. Dust these bars with a little powdered sugar to add extra sweetness and balance the tartness of the lemon. *Nut-free*

PREP TIME: 10 minutes
COOK TIME: 40 minutes, plus 2 hours to chill

FOR THE SHORTBREAD CRUST

2 cups all-purpose flour

½ cup granulated sugar

1 cup (2 sticks) unsalted butter, room temperature

FOR THE FILLING

1½ cups granulated sugar

⅓ cup all-purpose flour

4 large eggs, room temperature

⅔ cup freshly squeezed lemon juice

1 tablespoon grated lemon zest

Powdered sugar, for topping

TO MAKE THE SHORTBREAD CRUST

1. **Preheat the oven.** Preheat the oven to 350°F. Lightly coat a 9-by-13-inch baking pan with cooking spray or line with parchment paper.

2. **Make the crust.** In a large bowl, whisk together the flour and sugar. Incorporate the butter into the flour mixture until it resembles coarse crumbs. Press the dough into the pan to form an even crust and bake for 20 minutes, or until the edges of the crust are lightly browned.

TO MAKE THE FILLING

1. **Make the filling.** In the same bowl you used for the crust, whisk together the sugar, flour, eggs, lemon juice, and lemon zest.

2. **Pour the filling over the crust.** When the crust is done, remove it from the oven and immediately pour the lemon filling over the hot crust.

3. **Finish baking.** Bake for another 20 minutes, until the filling is set. Dust the top of the lemon bars with powdered sugar. Set the pan on a wire rack and cool for 20 minutes, then transfer to the refrigerator to chill and set, about 2 hours.

SUBSTITUTION TIP: To switch up the filling, use orange, lime, or even grapefruit juice and zest.

Pecan Pie Bars

Makes 16 bars

This is a fabulous recipe to make for the holidays, and
it's exponentially easier than making a pie.

PREP TIME: **10 minutes**
COOK TIME: **45 minutes**

FOR THE CRUST

2 cups all-purpose flour

⅓ cup granulated sugar

¼ teaspoon salt

11 tablespoons unsalted
butter

FOR THE FILLING

3 large eggs, room
temperature

1 cup light corn syrup

½ cup granulated sugar

½ cup light brown sugar

2 tablespoons unsalted
butter, melted

1 teaspoon vanilla extract

2½ cups chopped pecans

TO MAKE THE CRUST

1. Preheat the oven. Preheat the oven to 350°F. Lightly
coat a 9-by-13-inch baking pan with cooking spray or
line with parchment paper.

2. Make the crust. In a large bowl, whisk together the
flour, sugar, and salt. Cut the butter into the flour mixture until it resembles cornmeal. Press the dough into
the pan to form an even crust and bake for 20 minutes.

TO MAKE THE FILLING

1. Make the filling. In a large bowl, mix together the
eggs, corn syrup, granulated sugar, brown sugar, butter,
and vanilla until smooth. Stir in the pecans. Spread the
filling evenly over the crust.

2. Finish baking. Bake for 25 minutes, or until set. Set
the pan on a wire rack and cool completely before cutting into bars.

SUBSTITUTION TIP: Try stirring in 1 cup of semisweet chocolate chips with the pecans when you make
the filling.

Apple Pie Bars

Makes 9 to 12 bars

Combining everything you love about apple pie in one easy, breezy bar, these bars just might replace your grandmother's top-secret apple pie recipe. *Nut-free*

PREP TIME: **20 minutes**
COOK TIME: **50 minutes,
plus 20 minutes to cool and
2 hours to chill**

FOR THE CRUST

2 cups all-purpose flour

½ cup granulated sugar

½ teaspoon salt

**14 tablespoons (1¾ sticks)
unsalted butter, melted
and slightly cooled**

FOR THE FILLING

**3 large apples, peeled,
cored, and thinly sliced
(about ¼-inch thick)**

**6 tablespoons granulated
sugar**

**2 teaspoons ground
cinnamon**

**6 tablespoons
all-purpose flour**

**½ teaspoon ground
nutmeg**

FOR THE STREUSEL

½ cup light brown sugar

½ cup all-purpose flour

**¼ cup quick cooking or
old-fashioned oats**

**4 tablespoons (½ stick)
unsalted butter,
room temperature**

TO MAKE THE CRUST

1. **Preheat the oven.** Preheat the oven to 350°F degrees. Lightly coat a 9-by-13-inch baking pan with cooking spray or line with parchment paper.

2. **Make the crust.** In a small bowl, combine the flour, sugar, and salt. Add the melted butter and stir to combine. Press the dough into the pan to form an even crust and bake for 20 minutes.

TO MAKE THE FILLING

Make the filling. In a large bowl, combine all the filling ingredients and mix well. Spread the filling over the baked crust.

TO MAKE THE STREUSEL

1. **Make the streusel.** In a medium bowl, combine the sugar, flour, and oats. Incorporate the butter until the dough is crumbly. Sprinkle the topping over the apples.

2. **Finish baking.** Bake for 30 minutes, or until the streusel is golden brown. Set the pan on a wire rack and cool for 20 minutes, then refrigerate for about 2 hours.

SUBSTITUTION TIP: Try replacing the apples with sliced peaches or strawberries.

Raspberry Jam Bars

Makes 12 bars

Layered with sweet raspberry jam, these hearty oatmeal bars are
a foolproof recipe and come together in minutes. *Nut-free*

PREP TIME: 10 minutes
COOK TIME: 40 minutes

1 cup all-purpose flour

1 cup old-fashioned rolled
oats

½ cup light brown sugar

¼ teaspoon baking soda

¼ teaspoon ground
cinnamon

¼ teaspoon salt

8 tablespoons (1 stick)
unsalted butter,
room temperature

1 cup raspberry jam

1. **Preheat the oven.** Preheat the oven to 350°F. Lightly coat an 8-by-8-inch baking pan with cooking spray or line with parchment paper.

2. **Combine the dry ingredients.** In a small bowl, whisk together the flour, oats, sugar, baking soda, cinnamon, and salt.

3. **Add the butter.** Incorporate the butter into the dry ingredients to form a crumbly mixture.

4. **Prepare the bottom crust.** Put 2 cups of the oat mixture into the bottom of the pan and press it down in an even layer.

5. **Add the jam.** Put the jam in a microwave-safe container and warm for 15 to 30 seconds to make it easier to spread. Spread the jam over the crust to within ¼ inch of the edge.

6. **Add the top crust.** Sprinkle the remaining oat mixture over the top and lightly press it into the jam.

7. **Bake.** Bake for 35 to 40 minutes, or until lightly browned. Set the pan on a wire rack and cool completely before cutting into bars.

SUBSTITUTION TIP: If you don't have old-fashioned oats on hand, quick oats will also work.

Raspberry Cheesecake Brownies

Makes 12 brownies

Fudgy brownies just got a little better with a sweet
raspberry cheesecake topping! *Nut-free*

PREP TIME: 20 minutes
**COOK TIME: 25 minutes, plus
2 hours to cool**

FOR THE TOPPING

1 cup cream cheese,
    room temperature

⅓ cup granulated sugar

1 teaspoon vanilla extract

1 large egg, room
    temperature

¼ cup raspberry jam

FOR THE BROWNIES

8 tablespoons (1 stick)
    unsalted butter,
    melted and slightly
    cooled

½ cup unsweetened
    cocoa powder

⅔ cup granulated sugar

⅓ cup light brown sugar

2 large eggs, room
    temperature

1 teaspoon vanilla extract

1 cup all-purpose flour

½ teaspoon salt

½ cup semisweet
    chocolate chips
    (optional)

TO MAKE THE TOPPING

1. Preheat the oven. Preheat the oven to 375°F. Lightly coat an 8-by-8-inch baking pan with cooking spray or line with parchment paper.

2. Make the cheesecake topping. In a medium bowl, using an electric mixer, mix together the cream cheese and sugar. Add the vanilla and egg and mix until combined.

TO MAKE THE BROWNIES

1. Combine the butter, cocoa powder, and sugars. In a large bowl, mix together the butter, cocoa powder, granulated sugar, and brown sugar.

2. Add the eggs and vanilla. Allow to cool slightly before adding the eggs, one at a time, mixing well after each addition. Mix in the vanilla.

3. Add the dry ingredients. Stir in the flour and salt, just until incorporated. Stir in the chocolate chips, if using.

4. Spread the batter into the pan. Spread the brownie batter in the pan in an even layer. Spread the cheesecake topping on top of the brownie batter. Add the raspberry jam to the cheesecake topping and swirl with a knife.

5. Bake. Bake for 20 to 25 minutes, or until the top is set. Set the pan on a wire rack and cool completely, about 2 hours, before cutting the bars.

SUBSTITUTION TIP: Top the brownies with ½ cup of fresh raspberries before baking.

5

Perfect Pies, Galettes, Tarts, and Quiches

Basic Pie Dough with Sweet
Pie Dough Option 60

Key Lime Pie 61

Brownie Pie 62

Chocolate Pecan Pie 63

Apple Streusel Pie 64

Cranberry-Pear Crumble Pie 65

Blueberry Crumble Pie 66

Praline Pumpkin Pie 68

Fresh Cherry Pie 70

Chocolate Cream Pie 72

Black Bottom Peanut
Butter Mousse Pie 74

Banana Cream Pie 76

Coconut Cream Pie 78

Lemon Meringue Pie 80

Strawberry-Rhubarb Galette 82

Mixed Berry Galette 83

Caprese Galette 85

Peach-Blueberry Tart 86

Lemon Cheesecake Tart 87

Berry White Chocolate Tart 88

Summer Vegetable Tart 89

Bacon and Swiss Quiche 91

Mushroom Quiche 92

Sausage and Spinach Quiche 93

Basic Pie Dough with Sweet Pie Dough Option

Makes 1 (9- to 14-inch) crust

Making your own pie crust is easy and worth it in the end. I use all butter, so the crust is flaky and flavorful. This recipe makes a single crust, but for a double crust pie—like Fresh Cherry Pie (page 70)—simply double the recipe, and in step 2, form the dough into two 4-inch disks, then proceed as directed. *Nut-free*

PREP TIME: 15 minutes, plus 1 hour to chill

1¼ cups all-purpose flour

½ teaspoon salt

8 tablespoons (1 stick) unsalted butter, chilled and cut into cubes

3 to 4 tablespoons ice water

1. **Make the dough.** In a medium bowl, combine the flour and salt. Cut in the butter until the texture resembles coarse cornmeal. Sprinkle in 3 tablespoons of the ice water. Using a rubber spatula, stir the dough until it sticks together. If it does not stick together, add the remaining 1 tablespoon of water.

2. **Refrigerate the dough.** Turn the dough out onto a sheet of plastic wrap and flatten it into a 4-inch disk. Tightly wrap the dough and refrigerate for at least 1 hour and up to 3 days. You can also freeze the dough for up to 3 months for later use. Before you are ready to use the frozen dough, remove it from the freezer and allow it to thaw in the refrigerator for 24 hours.

PREPARATION TIP: To make Sweet Pie Dough, mix in 1 tablespoon of granulated sugar with the flour and salt in step 1, then proceed as directed.

Key Lime Pie

Makes 1 (9-inch) pie

The first time I tasted Key lime pie, I was in heaven. I was shocked to learn that the recipe came from the back of a condensed milk can. This superbly simple version comes together in minutes. *Nut-free*

PREP TIME: 10 minutes
COOK TIME: 20 minutes,
plus 1 hour to chill

FOR THE CRUST

1½ cups graham cracker crumbs

6 tablespoons (¾ stick) unsalted butter, melted

⅓ cup granulated sugar

⅛ teaspoon salt

FOR THE FILLING

2 (15-ounce) cans sweetened condensed milk

½ cup (4 ounces) full-fat sour cream

¾ cup freshly squeezed Key lime juice

2 teaspoons grated lime zest

TO MAKE THE CRUST

1. **Preheat the oven.** Position a rack in the middle of the oven. Preheat the oven to 350°F.

2. **Make the crust.** In a medium bowl, mix together the graham cracker crumbs, butter, sugar, and salt. Put the mixture in a 9-inch pie pan and press it into the bottom and up the sides to make an even crust. Bake for 8 minutes, or until set and golden. Set aside on a wire rack. Leave the oven on.

TO MAKE THE FILLING

1. **Make the filling.** In a medium bowl, combine all the ingredients for the filling. Pour the filling into the graham cracker crust.

2. **Finish baking.** Bake for 8 to 10 minutes, or until the filling is set.

3. **Chill.** Refrigerate the pie for at least 1 hour and up to 3 days before serving.

INGREDIENT TIP: Fresh Key limes can be difficult to find, so feel free to use bottled Key lime juice.

Brownie Pie

Makes 1 (9-inch) pie

If you offered me a brownie or a slice of pie, I'd have a hard time choosing. Thanks to this two-in-one option, I don't have to. *Nut-free*

PREP TIME: 20 minutes
COOK TIME: 45 minutes, plus 1 to 2 hours to cool

FOR THE CRUST

Sweet Pie Dough
  (page 60)

FOR THE BROWNIE

8 tablespoons (1 stick)
  unsalted butter,
  melted

1 cup granulated sugar

2 large eggs, room
  temperature

1 teaspoon vanilla extract

½ cup unsweetened
  cocoa powder

½ cup all-purpose flour

¼ teaspoon salt

¼ teaspoon baking
  powder

1 cup semisweet
  chocolate chips

TO MAKE THE CRUST

Roll out the dough. Place the pie dough on a lightly floured work surface. Using a rolling pin, roll out the dough into a 12-inch circle. Place the dough into a 9-inch pie dish. Leave a 1-inch overhang around the edge. Trim off any excess dough. Fold the overhang underneath itself around the edge, crimping as you go. Refrigerate the crust as you make the filling.

TO MAKE THE BROWNIE

1. Preheat the oven. Preheat the oven to 350°F.

2. Make the brownie batter. In a large bowl, mix together the butter, sugar, eggs, and vanilla. Using a rubber spatula, stir in the cocoa powder, flour, salt, and baking powder. Stir in the chocolate chips. Pour the batter into the crust.

3. Bake. Place the pie pan on a baking sheet. Bake for 40 to 45 minutes, or until the top is cracked. Do not overbake. Set the pie dish on a wire rack to cool for 1 to 2 hours.

SUBSTITUTION TIP: For a little crunch, stir in 1 cup of toasted, chopped nuts, like pecans or walnuts.

Chocolate Pecan Pie

Makes 1 (9-inch) pie

In my opinion, the only thing missing from a pecan pie is chocolate. Remedying that, this recipe incorporates a simple brown sugar filling that gets poured over the pecans and chocolate chunks.

PREP TIME: **30 minutes**
COOK TIME: **50 minutes, plus 3 hours to cool**

FOR THE CRUST
Sweet Pie Dough (page 60)

FOR THE FILLING
6 tablespoons (¾ stick) unsalted butter, melted

1 cup light brown sugar

¾ cup light corn syrup

1 teaspoon vanilla extract

¼ teaspoon salt

3 large eggs, room temperature

2 cups pecan halves

1 cup semisweet chocolate chunks

TO MAKE THE CRUST

Roll out the dough. Place the dough on a lightly floured work surface. Using a rolling pin, roll out the dough into a 12-inch circle. Place the dough into a 9-inch pie dish. Leave a 1-inch overhang around the edge. Trim off any excess dough. Fold the overhang underneath, crimping the edges.

TO MAKE THE FILLING

1. Preheat the oven. Position a rack in the lower third of the oven. Preheat the oven to 350°F.

2. Make the filling. In a medium bowl, whisk together the butter and brown sugar until smooth. Whisk in the corn syrup, vanilla, and salt. In a separate medium bowl, lightly beat the eggs, then whisk in the brown sugar mixture. Arrange the pecans and chocolate chunks on the bottom crust. Pour the brown sugar filling over the pecans and chocolate.

3. Bake. Place the pie on a large baking sheet and bake for 40 to 50 minutes, or until the filling is set. Set the pie dish on a wire rack to cool for 3 hours.

SUBSTITUTION TIP: You can use bittersweet chocolate chips, or 6 ounces of chopped bittersweet or dark chocolate.

Apple Streusel Pie

Makes 1 (9-inch) pie

Growing up, one of my favorite desserts was apple streusel pie purchased from a local orchard. Like those beloved pies, this recipe has a buttery crust, spiced apple filling, and festive cinnamon brown sugar streusel on top. *Nut-free*

PREP TIME: 2 hours
COOK TIME: 55 minutes, plus 3 hours to cool

FOR THE CRUST
Sweet Pie Dough (page 60)

FOR THE FILLING
3 pounds apples, peeled, cored, and cut into ¼-inch-thick slices (about 6 large apples)

1 tablespoon freshly squeezed lemon juice

¾ cup granulated sugar

3 tablespoons all-purpose flour

¼ teaspoon salt

2 teaspoons ground cinnamon

½ teaspoon nutmeg

FOR THE STREUSEL
1 cup all-purpose flour

⅔ cup light brown sugar

1 teaspoon ground cinnamon

¼ teaspoon salt

8 tablespoons (1 stick) unsalted butter, chilled and cut into cubes

TO MAKE THE CRUST

Roll out the dough. Place the pie dough on a lightly floured work surface. Using a rolling pin, roll out the dough into a 12-inch circle. Place the dough into a 9-inch pie dish. Leave a 1-inch overhang around the edge. Trim off any excess dough. Fold the overhang underneath itself around the edge, crimping as you go.

TO MAKE THE FILLING

Make the filling. In a large bowl, using a rubber spatula, mix together the apples, lemon juice, sugar, flour, salt, cinnamon, and nutmeg. Spoon the filling into the crust, leaving some of the liquid in the bowl. Refrigerate the pie while making the streusel topping.

TO MAKE THE STREUSEL

1. Preheat the oven. Position a rack in the lower third of the oven. Preheat the oven to 400°F.

2. Make the streusel. In a large bowl, combine the flour, sugar, cinnamon, and salt. Cut in the butter until thick and crumbly. Sprinkle the streusel topping over the apples.

3. Bake. Place the pie pan on a baking sheet in the lower third of the oven and bake for 20 minutes. Reduce the temperature to 375°F and bake for 30 to 35 minutes more. Set the pie dish on a wire rack and cool for 3 hours.

TROUBLESHOOTING TIP: If the streusel topping is browning too quickly, cover the top of the pie with foil.

Cranberry-Pear Crumble Pie

Makes 1 (9-inch) pie

In this recipe, juicy pears are tossed with cinnamon and tart cranberries, then topped with a crunchy oatmeal streusel, resulting in a pie that might just take center stage at your holiday table. *Nut-free*

PREP TIME: **30 minutes**
COOK TIME: **55 minutes, plus 3 hours to cool**

FOR THE CRUST
Sweet Pie Dough
   (page 60)

FOR THE FILLING
5 cups pears, peeled, cored, and diced into ½-inch chunks (4 to 5 pears)

1 tablespoon freshly squeezed lemon juice

⅓ cup all-purpose flour

½ cup granulated sugar

1½ teaspoons ground cinnamon

1¾ cups cranberries, fresh or frozen

FOR THE TOPPING
1 cup all-purpose flour

¾ cup light brown sugar

⅓ cup granulated sugar

½ teaspoon ground cinnamon

¼ teaspoon salt

8 tablespoons (1 stick) unsalted butter, melted

½ cup old-fashioned oats

TO MAKE THE CRUST

Roll out the dough. Place the pie dough on a lightly floured work surface. Using a rolling pin, roll out the dough into a 12-inch circle. Place the dough into a 9-inch pie dish. Leave a 1-inch overhang around the edge. Trim off any excess dough. Fold the overhang underneath itself around the edges, crimping as you go.

TO MAKE THE FILLING

Make the filling. In a large bowl, gently mix together all the filling ingredients until combined. Spoon the filling into the crust. Refrigerate the pie while making the topping.

TO MAKE THE TOPPING

1. Preheat the oven. Position a rack in the lower third of the oven. Preheat the oven to 400°F.

2. Make the topping. In a medium bowl, combine the flour, brown sugar, granulated sugar, cinnamon, and salt. Incorporate the butter until the topping has a crumbly texture. Stir in the oats. Sprinkle the topping over the filling.

3. Bake. Place the pie pan on a baking sheet in the lower third of the oven and bake for 20 minutes. Reduce the temperature to 375°F and bake for 30 to 35 minutes more. Set the pie dish on a wire rack to cool for 3 hours.

INGREDIENT TIP: I used green Anjou pears for this pie, but you could also use Bosc or Bartlett pears.

Blueberry Crumble Pie

Makes 1 (9-inch) pie

My brother and father are huge fans of blueberry pie, but
I've never loved it as much as they do. That is, until I added a
brown sugar cinnamon crumble to the top. *Nut-free*

PREP TIME: 40 minutes
**COOK TIME: 1 hour 5 minutes,
plus 3 hours to cool**

FOR THE CRUST

Basic Pie Dough
(page 60)

**FOR THE BLUEBERRY
FILLING**

6 cups blueberries,
divided, fresh or frozen

1 apple, peeled, cored,
and grated

2 teaspoons grated
lemon zest

2 teaspoons freshly
squeezed lemon juice

¾ cup granulated sugar

2 tablespoons cornstarch

⅛ teaspoon salt

TO MAKE THE CRUST

Roll out the dough. Place the pie dough on a lightly
floured work surface. Using a rolling pin, roll out the
dough into a 12-inch circle. Place the dough into a
9-inch pie dish. Leave a 1-inch overhang around the
edge. Trim off any excess dough. Fold the overhang
underneath around the edges, crimping as you go.

TO MAKE THE BLUEBERRY FILLING

1. Cook down the blueberries. Place 3 cups of berries
in a medium saucepan set over medium heat. Mash
the berries to release their juices. Cook, stirring frequently, until half of the berries have broken down and
the mixture is thickened and reduced to 1½ cups, about
8 minutes. Let cool.

2. Make the filling. In a large bowl, mix together the
cooked berries and the remaining berries along with
the apple, lemon zest, lemon juice, sugar, cornstarch,
and salt.

FOR THE CRUMBLE TOPPING

- ¾ cup all-purpose flour
- 3 tablespoons light brown sugar
- ½ teaspoon ground cinnamon
- ¼ teaspoon salt
- 5 tablespoons unsalted butter, melted and cooled slightly

TO MAKE THE CRUMBLE TOPPING AND ASSEMBLE THE PIE

1. **Preheat the oven.** Position a rack in the lower third of the oven. Preheat the oven to 400°F.

2. **Make the topping.** In a medium bowl, combine the flour, sugar, cinnamon, and salt. Pour in the butter. Stir to combine.

3. **Assemble the pie.** Pour the filling into the crust. Sprinkle the crumble topping over the top.

4. **Bake.** Place the pie pan on a baking sheet in the lower third of the oven and bake for 20 minutes. Reduce the temperature to 375°F and bake for 30 to 35 minutes more. Set the pie dish on a wire rack to cool for 3 hours.

SUBSTITUTION TIP: Feel free to make this pie crust with the Sweet Pie Dough option.

Praline Pumpkin Pie

Makes 1 (9-inch) pie

I was never a big fan of plain pumpkin pie, so I jazz it up
by adding a crunchy cinnamon pecan topping.

**PREP TIME: 20 minutes, plus
30 minutes to chill**
COOK TIME:
**1 hour 25 minutes, plus
2 hours to cool**

FOR THE CRUST
Sweet Pie Dough
(page 60)

FOR THE FILLING
1 (15-ounce) can
sweetened condensed
milk
1 (15-ounce) can
pumpkin purée
2 tablespoons cornstarch
2 teaspoons pumpkin
pie spice
1 teaspoon vanilla extract

TO MAKE THE CRUST

1. Roll out the dough. Place the pie dough on a lightly
floured work surface. Using a rolling pin, roll out the
dough into a 12-inch circle. Place the dough into a 9-inch
pie dish. Leave a 1-inch overhang around the edge. Trim
off any excess dough. Fold the overhang underneath
itself around the edges, crimping as you go. Refrigerate
for 30 minutes.

2. Blind-bake. Preheat the oven to 400°F. Line the dough
with parchment paper or foil. Fill with pie weights or
dried beans. Bake for about 15 minutes, or until the edges
begin to brown. Remove the parchment and weights.
Prick the crust with a fork. Bake for about 7 minutes
more, or until the bottom crust is golden brown. Remove
from the oven and allow to cool. Lower the oven temperature to 375°F.

TO MAKE THE FILLING

Make the filling. In a large bowl, combine the condensed milk, pumpkin purée, cornstarch, pumpkin
spice, and vanilla. Whisk until smooth. Pour the filling
into the pie shell.

FOR THE TOPPING

¼ cup light brown sugar

4 tablespoons (½ stick) unsalted butter, room temperature

⅔ cup toasted chopped pecans

⅛ teaspoon salt

¼ teaspoon ground cinnamon

¼ cup all-purpose flour

TO MAKE THE TOPPING

1. **Make the topping.** In a small bowl, mix together all the topping ingredients until well combined. Sprinkle over the filling.

2. **Bake.** Bake for 50 minutes to 1 hour, or until the pie appears firm and a knife comes out clean. Set the pie dish on a wire rack to cool for 2 hours.

SUBSTITUTION TIP: If you don't have pumpkin pie spice in your cupboard, make your own. Combine 1 teaspoon of cinnamon, ¼ teaspoon of cloves, ½ teaspoon of ginger, and ¼ teaspoon of nutmeg.

Fresh Cherry Pie

Makes 1 (9-inch) pie

This delicious pie is nothing like the cherry pies made with canned filling I had as a child. Splashes of vanilla and almond extract bring nuanced flavors to this summer classic.

PREP TIME: 2 hours

COOK TIME: 1 hour 5 minutes, plus 3 hours to cool

FOR THE CRUST

2 recipes Basic Pie Dough (page 60)

1 large egg, beaten, for the egg wash

1 tablespoon water, for the egg wash

Coarse turbinado sugar, for topping

FOR THE FILLING

5 cups cherries, pitted and halved

¾ cup granulated sugar

3 tablespoons cornstarch

½ teaspoon salt

¼ teaspoon almond extract

1 teaspoon vanilla extract

1 tablespoon freshly squeezed lemon juice

2 tablespoons unsalted butter, cut into cubes

TO MAKE THE CRUST

1. Roll out the crust. Remove one 4-inch disk of pie dough from the refrigerator. Lightly flour a clean work surface. Roll the disk into a 12-inch circle. Place into a 9-inch pie dish. Leave a 1-inch overhang around the edge. Trim off any excess dough. Reserve the second disk of dough until after you fill the pie.

2. Make the egg wash. Beat together the egg and water until well combined.

TO MAKE THE FILLING AND ASSEMBLE THE PIE

1. Preheat the oven. Position a rack in the lower third of the oven. Preheat the oven to 425°F.

2. Make the filling. In a large bowl, stir together the cherries, sugar, cornstarch, salt, almond extract, vanilla, and lemon juice. Spoon the filling into the crust, leaving some of the liquid in the bowl. Scatter the butter over the filling.

3. Add the top crust. Remove the second 4-inch disk of pie dough from the refrigerator and place it on a lightly floured surface. Roll it into a 12-inch circle. Place it over the filling, leaving a 1-inch overhang around the edge. Trim off any excess dough. Working around the edge, fold the top and bottom overhang under, crimping the edges as you go. Cut a few slits in the top crust to allow steam to escape. Lightly brush the crust with the egg wash. Sprinkle the coarse sugar over the top.

4. **Bake.** Place the pie pan on a baking sheet in the lower third of the oven and bake for 15 minutes. Reduce the temperature to 350°F and bake 45 to 50 minutes more, or until the crust is golden brown and the filling is bubbling. Cover the edges of the pie with foil if they are browning too quickly. Set the pie dish on a wire rack to cool for 3 hours.

SUBSTITUTION TIP: You can also use frozen cherries. Thaw them before using and be sure to drain any excess liquid, as it will seep into the pie dough.

Chocolate Cream Pie

Makes 1 (9-inch) pie

With its silky chocolate pudding filling and devilishly sweet
chocolate cookie crust, this classic diner pie is exactly what
every chocolate lover—like me—craves. *Nut-free*

**PREP TIME: 45 minutes,
30 minutes to chill**
**COOK TIME: 10 minutes, plus
6 hours to chill and set**

FOR THE CRUST

24 chocolate sandwich
cookies

5 tablespoons unsalted
butter, melted

⅛ teaspoon salt

FOR THE FILLING

4 large egg yolks, beaten

1½ cups granulated sugar

4 tablespoons cornstarch

½ cup unsweetened
cocoa powder

½ teaspoon salt

3 cups whole milk

2 tablespoons
unsalted butter,
room temperature

1½ teaspoons vanilla
extract

TO MAKE THE CRUST

Make the crust. Add the cookies to a food processor
and pulse until they become crumbs or place them in a
sealable plastic bag and crush them with a rolling pin.
In a medium bowl, combine the cookie crumbs, butter,
and salt. Put the crust mixture into a 9-inch pie pan and
press it into the bottom and up the sides of the pan to
make an even crust. Refrigerate for 30 minutes.

TO MAKE THE FILLING

1. Make the filling. In a large heavy-duty saucepan
over medium heat, whisk together the egg yolks and
sugar. Whisk in the cornstarch, cocoa powder, and salt.
Add the milk and whisk gently.

2. Cook the filling. Cook over medium heat, stirring
constantly, until the pudding comes to a boil and has
thickened, about 10 minutes. Remove from the heat.
Stir in the butter and vanilla. Cool slightly, then pour
the pudding into the pie crust. Cover the pie with
plastic wrap to prevent a pudding skin from forming.
Refrigerate for 4 to 6 hours, or until set.

FOR THE WHIPPED CREAM

1 cup cold heavy cream

3 tablespoons powdered sugar

1 teaspoon vanilla extract

TO MAKE THE WHIPPED CREAM

Make the whipped cream. Using an electric mixer fitted with a whisk attachment and set on medium-high, beat the cream, powdered sugar, and vanilla until stiff peaks form, about 5 minutes. Spread or pipe onto the chilled pie before serving.

SUBSTITUTION TIP: You can also make this with a traditional pie crust. Follow the directions to make the custard and chill it in a separate bowl. Make your pie crust, blind-bake it, and cool it completely before adding the chilled filling.

Black Bottom Peanut Butter Mousse Pie

Makes 1 (9-inch) pie

This pie conceals a layer of chocolate beneath a
creamy peanut butter mousse filling.

**PREP TIME: 40 minutes, plus
4 to 6 hours to chill**

FOR THE CRUST

24 chocolate sandwich
cookies

5 tablespoons unsalted
butter, melted

⅛ teaspoon salt

FOR THE FUDGE
LAYER

½ cup semisweet
chocolate chips

¼ cup heavy cream

1 tablespoon
unsalted butter,
room temperature

¼ teaspoon vanilla
extract

TO MAKE THE CRUST

Make the crust. Place the cookies in a food processor
and pulse into crumbs. Or, place them in a sealable
plastic bag and crush them with a rolling pin. In a
medium bowl, mix together the cookie crumbs, butter,
and salt. Put the crust mixture into a 9-inch pie pan and
press it into the bottom and up the sides of the pan to
make an even crust. Refrigerate for 30 minutes.

TO MAKE THE FUDGE LAYER

Make the fudge layer. In a microwave-safe bowl,
combine all the ingredients for the fudge layer. Microwave in 30-second intervals, stirring in between each
interval, until the chocolate is melted and smooth. Pour
into the crust. Freeze for 10 minutes until firm.

FOR THE MOUSSE FILLING

1 cup cream cheese, room temperature

⅔ cup powdered sugar

¾ cup smooth peanut butter

1 teaspoon vanilla extract

¾ cup cold heavy cream

TO MAKE THE MOUSSE FILLING

1. **Make the filling**. In a medium bowl, using an electric mixer set on medium, mix together the cream cheese and sugar until light and fluffy. Mix in the peanut butter and vanilla.

2. **Whip the cream.** In a separate medium bowl, using an electric mixer fitted with a whisk attachment and set on medium-high, whip the cold cream until soft peaks form, 2 to 3 minutes. Fold the whipped cream into the peanut butter mixture.

3. **Finish assembling.** Spread the mousse over the fudge layer. Cover the pie with plastic wrap and chill for 4 to 6 hours.

SUBSTITUTION TIP: For added pizzazz, sprinkle chocolate chips, toasted peanuts, or even chopped peanut butter cups over the top.

Banana Cream Pie

Makes 1 (9-inch) pie

Traditionally, the creamy vanilla custard and fresh bananas in this pie are set in a regular pie crust. This recipe uses a quick and easy cookie crust. *Nut-free*

PREP TIME: 45 minutes
COOK TIME: 30 minutes, plus 10 minutes to cool and 1 hour to chill

FOR THE CRUST

1½ cups vanilla wafer or graham cracker crumbs

6 tablespoons (¾ stick) unsalted butter, melted

⅓ cup granulated sugar

⅛ teaspoon salt

FOR THE FILLING

4 egg yolks

¾ cup granulated sugar

⅓ cup cornstarch

¼ teaspoon salt

2 cups whole milk

2 tablespoons unsalted butter, room temperature

1¼ teaspoons vanilla extract

2 to 3 bananas, peeled and sliced

TO MAKE THE CRUST

1. Preheat the oven. Preheat the oven to 350°F. Lightly coat a 9-inch pie pan with cooking spray.

2. Make the crust. In a medium bowl, combine all the ingredients for the crust. Put the crust mixture into the pie pan and press it into the bottom and up the sides of the pan to make an even crust. Bake for 10 minutes. Cool completely before filling.

TO MAKE THE FILLING

1. Make the filling. In a small bowl, beat the egg yolks and set aside. In a medium saucepan, combine the sugar, cornstarch, and salt. Add the milk gradually while stirring gently. Cook over medium heat, stirring constantly, until the mixture comes to a boil, about 10 minutes. Continue to whisk and cook for about 2 more minutes more. Remove from the heat.

2. Temper the eggs. Stir a small quantity of the hot mixture into the beaten egg yolks, then immediately add egg yolk mixture to the rest of the hot filling. Return the pan to the heat and cook, whisking constantly, for about 2 minutes. Remove the pan from the heat, then add the butter and vanilla. Stir until the butter is melted and the consistency is smooth.

3. Add the bananas. Arrange the bananas on the bottom crust. Pour the custard over the bananas. Allow to cool for 10 minutes, then cover the pie with plastic wrap to prevent a pudding skin from forming. Refrigerate for 1 hour.

FOR THE WHIPPED CREAM

1 cup cold heavy cream

3 tablespoons powdered sugar

1 teaspoon vanilla extract

TO MAKE THE WHIPPED CREAM

Make the whipped cream. Using an electric mixer fitted with a whisk attachment and set on medium-high, beat the cream, powdered sugar, and vanilla until stiff peaks form, about 5 minutes. Spread or pipe onto the chilled pie before serving.

TROUBLESHOOTING TIP: By tempering the egg yolks, you are slowly raising the temperature of the eggs so they don't curdle. This step ensures that you get a smooth filling.

Coconut Cream Pie

Makes 1 (9-inch) pie

I didn't discover coconut cream pie until I was a server at a diner during
my college years, but once I did, I couldn't get enough! *Nut-free*

PREP TIME: **45 minutes, plus
30 minutes to chill**
COOK TIME: **45 minutes,
plus 10 minutes to cool and
4 hours to chill and set**

FOR THE CRUST
Sweet Pie Dough
(page 60)

**FOR THE COCONUT
FILLING**
4 large egg yolks, room
temperature

1½ cups heavy cream

1 (14-ounce) can coconut
milk

¾ cup granulated sugar

⅓ cup cornstarch

¼ teaspoon salt

2 tablespoons
unsalted butter,
room temperature

½ teaspoon vanilla
extract

1 teaspoon coconut
extract

1 cup shredded
sweetened coconut

TO MAKE THE CRUST

1. Roll out the dough. Place the pie dough on a lightly
floured work surface. Using a rolling pin, roll out the
dough into a 12-inch circle. Place the dough into a
9-inch pie dish. Leave a 1-inch overhang around the
edge. Trim off any excess dough. Fold the overhang
underneath itself around the edges, crimping as you go.
Refrigerate for 30 minutes.

2. Blind-bake. Preheat the oven to 400°F. Line the
dough with parchment paper or foil. Fill with pie
weights or dried beans. Bake for about 15 minutes, or
until the edges begin to brown. Remove the parchment
and weights. Prick the crust with a fork. Bake for about
15 minutes more, or until the bottom crust is golden
brown. Cool completely before filling.

TO MAKE THE FILLING AND ASSEMBLE THE PIE

1. Make the filling. In a small bowl, beat the egg yolks
and set aside. In a medium saucepan, combine the
cream, coconut milk, sugar, cornstarch, and salt and
mix well. Cook over medium heat, stirring constantly,
until the mixture comes to a boil, about 10 minutes.
Continue to whisk and cook for about 2 minutes more.
Remove from the heat.

2. Temper the eggs. Stir a small quantity of the hot
mixture into the beaten egg yolks, then immediately
add the egg yolk mixture to the rest of the hot filling.
Return the pan to the heat, and cook, whisking constantly, for about 2 minutes. Remove the pan from the
heat, then add the butter, vanilla, and coconut extract

1 cup cold heavy cream

3 tablespoons powdered
sugar

1 teaspoon vanilla extract

and stir until the butter is melted and the consistency is smooth. Stir in the shredded coconut.

3. **Assemble the pie.** Pour the custard into the cooled pie crust. Allow to cool for 10 minutes, then cover the pie with plastic wrap to prevent a pudding skin from forming. Refrigerate for 4 hours, or until the filling is set.

TO MAKE THE WHIPPED CREAM

Make the whipped cream. Using an electric mixer fitted with a whisk attachment and set on medium-high, beat the cream, powdered sugar, and vanilla until stiff peaks form, about 5 minutes. Spread or pipe onto the chilled pie before serving.

INGREDIENT TIP: Use one can of full-fat coconut milk, not refrigerated coconut milk for this luscious pie.

Lemon Meringue Pie

Makes 1 (9-inch) pie

This dessert might be a labor of love with its pillowy meringue and tart filling, but it can be made successfully by a beginner baker like yourself. *Nut-free*

PREP TIME: 1 hour, plus 30 minutes to chill
COOK TIME: 55 minutes, plus 1 hour to cool and 4 hours to chill

FOR THE CRUST
Sweet Pie Dough (page 60)

FOR THE LEMON FILLING
4 large egg yolks, room temperature
1 cup granulated sugar
6 tablespoons cornstarch
¼ teaspoon salt
1½ cups water
½ cup freshly squeezed lemon juice
1 tablespoon grated lemon zest
2 tablespoons unsalted butter, room temperature

FOR THE MERINGUE
4 large egg whites, room temperature
¼ teaspoon cream of tartar
6 tablespoons granulated sugar

TO MAKE THE CRUST

1. Roll out the dough. Place the pie dough on a lightly floured work surface. Using a rolling pin, roll out the dough into a 12-inch circle. Place the dough into a 9-inch pie dish. Leave a 1-inch overhang around the edge. Trim off any excess dough. Fold the overhang underneath itself around the edges, crimping as you go. Refrigerate for 30 minutes.

2. Blind-bake. Preheat the oven to 400°F. Line the dough with parchment paper or foil. Fill with pie weights or dried beans. Bake for about 15 minutes, or until the edges begin to brown. Remove the parchment and weights. Prick the crust with a fork. Bake for about 7 minutes more, or until the bottom crust is golden brown. Set the pan on a wire rack to cool while you make the filling. Reduce the oven temperature to 350°F.

TO MAKE THE FILLING

1. Make the filling. In a small bowl, beat the egg yolks and set aside. In a medium saucepan, whisk together the sugar, cornstarch, salt, water, lemon juice, and lemon zest. Cook over medium heat, stirring constantly, until the mixture comes to a boil and visibly thickens, about 10 minutes. Continue to cook while whisking for 2 minutes more. Remove from the heat.

2. Temper the eggs. Stir a small quantity of the hot lemon mixture into the beaten egg yolks, then immediately add the egg yolk mixture to the rest of the hot lemon filling. Return the pan to the heat and cook, whisking constantly, for about 2 minutes. Remove the pan from the heat, then add the butter and stir until the butter has melted and the consistency is smooth. Pour the filling into the cooled pie crust.

TO MAKE THE MERINGUE

1. **Make the meringue.** In a large, dry bowl, using an electric mixer fitted with a whisk attachment set on high, whip the egg whites and cream of tartar together until soft peaks form, about 5 minutes. Add the sugar all at once. Continue beating on high speed until glossy stiff peaks form, about 2 more minutes. Spread the meringue on top of the warm filling, making sure it touches the crust.

2. **Bake.** Bake for 10 to 15 minutes, or until the meringue begins to brown. Set the pie dish on a wire rack to cool for 1 hour. Transfer the pie to the refrigerator and chill for 4 hours before slicing and serving. Lemon meringue pie is best enjoyed on the day it is made.

TROUBLESHOOTING TIP: Be sure there is no trace of egg yolk in the whites, which would keep them from whipping properly.

Strawberry-Rhubarb Galette

Makes 1 (12-inch) galette

My grandmother did not do a lot of baking, but every summer she would whip up a deliciously tart strawberry-rhubarb pie. This free-form galette is inspired by that pie and much easier to assemble. *Nut-free*

PREP TIME: **30 minutes, plus 1 hour to chill**
COOK TIME: **1 hour, plus 20 minutes to cool**

FOR THE CRUST

Sweet Pie Dough (page 60)

1 large egg, beaten, for the egg wash

1 tablespoon water, for the egg wash

Coarse turbinado sugar, for topping

FOR THE FILLING

3 tablespoons cornstarch

1½ cups rhubarb, sliced (about 3 stalks)

2 cups strawberries, sliced

½ teaspoon ground cinnamon

½ cup granulated sugar

¼ teaspoon salt

1 teaspoon freshly squeezed lemon juice

1 teaspoon vanilla extract

TO MAKE THE CRUST

1. Roll out the dough. Place the dough on a lightly floured work surface. Using a rolling pin, roll out the dough into a 14- to 15-inch circle.

2. Make the egg wash. Beat together the egg and water until combined.

TO MAKE THE FILLING AND ASSEMBLE THE GALETTE

1. Preheat the oven. Position a rack in the middle of the oven. Preheat the oven to 350°F. Line a baking sheet with parchment paper.

2. Make the filling. In a large bowl, mix together all the filling ingredients until thoroughly combined.

3. Form the galette. Place the dough on the baking sheet. Pour the fruit mixture onto the center of the dough, leaving a 2-inch border around the edge. Fold the border over the filling, leaving the center exposed and pleating the dough where necessary. Brush the crust sparingly with the egg wash and sprinkle with the coarse sugar.

4. Bake. Place the baking sheet on the middle rack and bake the galette for 1 hour, or until the crust is golden brown and the filling is bubbling. Transfer to a wire cooling rack to cool for at least 20 minutes.

INGREDIENT TIP: If using fresh rhubarb, cut the stalk into thin slices, and be sure to remove all the leaves. The leaves are poisonous and should not be consumed.

Mixed Berry Galette

Makes 1 (12-inch) galette

Growing up in rural upstate New York, we picked berries in our own backyard every summer. This galette is reminiscent of the berry pies we made with those fresh-picked berries. *Nut-free*

PREP TIME: 45 minutes, plus 30 minutes to chill
COOK TIME: 45 minutes, plus 20 minutes to cool

FOR THE CRUST

1½ cups all-purpose flour

¼ cup yellow cornmeal

1 tablespoon granulated sugar

½ teaspoon salt

8 tablespoons (1 stick) unsalted butter, chilled and cut into cubes

3 to 4 tablespoons cold buttermilk

1 large egg, beaten, for the egg wash

1 tablespoon of water, for the egg wash

Coarse turbinado sugar, for topping

TO MAKE THE CRUST

1. Make the dough. In a medium bowl, combine the flour, cornmeal, sugar, and salt. Cut in the butter until the texture resembles coarse cornmeal. Sprinkle in 3 tablespoons of the buttermilk. Using a rubber spatula, stir the dough until it sticks together. If it does not stick together, add the remaining 1 tablespoon of buttermilk.

2. Refrigerate the dough. Turn the dough out onto a sheet of plastic wrap and flatten it into a 4-inch disk. Tightly wrap it and refrigerate for 30 minutes.

3. Roll out the dough. Place the dough on a lightly floured work surface. Using a rolling pin, roll out the dough into a 14- or 15-inch circle.

4. Make the egg wash. Beat together the egg and water until combined.

Continued ▸

FOR THE FILLING

4 cups mixed berries, fresh or frozen

¼ cup granulated sugar

2 tablespoons all-purpose flour

1 tablespoon freshly squeezed lemon juice

½ teaspoon vanilla extract

TO MAKE THE FILLING AND ASSEMBLE THE GALETTE

1. **Preheat the oven.** Position a rack in the middle of the oven. Preheat the oven to 400°F. Line a baking sheet with parchment paper.

2. **Make the filling.** In a large bowl, gently mix together the berries, sugar, flour, lemon juice, and vanilla until thoroughly combined.

3. **Form the galette.** Place the dough on the baking sheet. Pour the fruit mixture onto the center of the dough, leaving a 2-inch border. Fold the border over the filling, leaving the center exposed and pleating the dough where necessary. Brush the crust sparingly with egg wash and sprinkle with the coarse sugar.

4. **Bake.** Place the baking sheet on the middle rack and bake the galette for about 45 minutes, or until the crust is golden brown and the filling is bubbling. Transfer to a wire cooling rack to cool for at least 20 minutes.

SUBSTITUTION TIP: If you don't have buttermilk, use ice water instead.

Caprese Galette

Makes 1 (12-inch) galette

I love a caprese salad in the summertime. This savory galette envelops tomato, mozzarella, and basil in a buttery crust sprinkled with Parmesan cheese. *Nut-free*

PREP TIME: **1 hour**
COOK TIME: **35 minutes, plus 20 minutes to cool**

FOR THE CRUST

Basic Pie Dough (page 60)

1 large egg, beaten, for the egg wash

1 tablespoon of water, for the egg wash

FOR THE FILLING

8 ounces fresh mozzarella, sliced

3 tomatoes, sliced

2 tablespoons grated Parmesan cheese

2 tablespoons olive oil

¼ cup minced fresh basil, for topping

TO MAKE THE CRUST

1. **Roll out the dough.** Place the pie dough on a lightly floured work surface. Using a rolling pin, roll out the dough into a 14- or 15-inch circle.

2. **Make the egg wash.** Beat together the egg and water until combined.

TO MAKE THE FILLING AND ASSEMBLE THE GALETTE

1. **Preheat the oven.** Position a rack in the middle of the oven. Preheat the oven to 400°F. Line a baking sheet with parchment paper.

2. **Form the galette.** Place the dough on the baking sheet. Arrange the mozzarella in the center, leaving a 2-inch border. Top with the sliced tomatoes. Fold the border over the filling, leaving the center exposed and pleating the dough where necessary. Brush the crust sparingly with the egg wash and sprinkle with Parmesan cheese. Drizzle the oil over the top.

3. **Bake.** Place the baking sheet on the middle rack and bake the galette for 30 to 35 minutes, or until the crust is golden brown and the filling is bubbling. Transfer to a wire cooling rack to cool for at least 20 minutes. Top with the basil.

TOPPING TIP: Try topping this galette with a drizzle of pesto or a balsamic reduction.

Peach-Blueberry Tart

Makes 1 (9-inch) tart

With a brown sugar crumble that is used for both the top and bottom crust, this tart has all the summer goodness of a peach pie but without the time commitment a traditional double-crust pie requires. *Nut-free*

PREP TIME: 10 minutes
COOK TIME: 45 minutes

3 cups all-purpose flour

1 cup light brown sugar

½ cup white granulated sugar

1 teaspoon salt

1½ teaspoons ground cinnamon

1 cup (2 sticks) unsalted butter, melted

1 cup blueberry jam

2 peaches, pitted and thinly sliced

1 cup blueberries

1. **Preheat the oven.** Position a rack in the middle of the oven. Preheat the oven to 375°F. Butter a 9-inch tart pan.

2. **Combine the dry ingredients.** In a large bowl, combine the flour, brown sugar, granulated sugar, salt, and cinnamon. Stir in the butter until the mixture forms moist crumbs. Place 2½ cups of the crumb mixture into the pan. Press it into the bottom and up the sides of the pan to form an even crust. Reserve the remaining crumb mixture.

3. **Add the remaining ingredients.** Spread the jam over the crust in an even layer. Top with the peaches and blueberries. Sprinkle the remaining crumb mixture over the fruit.

4. **Bake.** Bake until the topping is a deep golden brown, 35 to 45 minutes. Set the tart pan on a wire rack to cool for 20 minutes, then remove the sides and allow to cool completely.

SUBSTITUTION TIP: If you can't find blueberry jam, try using raspberry jam and fresh raspberries instead.

Lemon Cheesecake Tart

Makes 1 (9-inch) tart

With a buttery graham cracker crust and a simple lemon cheesecake filling, this tart is an elegant—and easy—dessert to serve guests. *Nut-free*

PREP TIME: 10 minutes

COOK TIME: 25 minutes, plus 2 hours to cool and 4 hours to chill

1½ cups graham cracker crumbs

6 tablespoons (¾ stick) unsalted butter, melted

¾ cup granulated sugar, divided

⅛ teaspoon salt

1 cup (8 ounces) cream cheese, room temperature

2 large eggs, room temperature

½ cup heavy cream

½ teaspoon vanilla extract

¼ cup freshly squeezed lemon juice

1 tablespoon grated lemon zest

1. **Preheat the oven.** Preheat the oven to 350°F.

2. **Make the crust.** In a medium bowl, mix together the graham cracker crumbs, butter, ¼ cup of the sugar, and salt until moist. Put the mixture in a 9-inch tart pan and press it into the bottom and up the sides of the pan to make an even crust.

3. **Make the filling.** In a large bowl, using an electric mixer set on medium, mix together the cream cheese and the remaining ½ cup sugar until smooth. Scrape down the bowl as needed. Add the eggs, one at a time, mixing well after each addition. Add the cream, vanilla, lemon juice, and lemon zest and mix until the filling is smooth. Pour the filling over the crust and smooth the top.

4. **Bake.** Bake for 20 to 25 minutes, or until set. Set the tart pan on a wire rack to cool to room temperature, 1 to 2 hours. Cover with plastic wrap and refrigerate about 4 hours, or until chilled.

SUBSTITUTION TIP: Replace the graham crackers with an equal amount of gingerbread cookie crumbs for an interesting twist on the crust.

Berry White Chocolate Tart

Makes 1 (9-inch) tart

With its velvety cheesecake filling and fresh berries, everyone will think you bought this tart at a fancy pastry shop. *Nut-free*

PREP TIME: **25 minutes, plus 1 hour to freeze**
COOK TIME: **35 minutes, plus 3 hours to chill**

FOR THE CRUST

1 egg yolk, room temperature

2 tablespoons ice water

¼ teaspoon vanilla extract

1¼ cups all-purpose flour

⅓ cup powdered sugar

¼ teaspoon salt

8 tablespoons (1 stick) unsalted butter, chilled and cut into cubes

FOR THE FILLING

1 cup (8 ounces) cream cheese

¼ cup cold heavy cream

⅓ cup powdered sugar

½ teaspoon vanilla extract

1 cup white chocolate chips, melted

2 cups mixed fresh berries

TO MAKE THE CRUST

1. Make the dough. In a small bowl, mix together the egg yolk, water, and vanilla and set aside. In a separate small bowl, combine the flour, sugar, and salt. Cut in the butter until the texture resembles coarse cornmeal. Add the egg mixture and mix with a fork until the dough begins to pull together.

2. Press the dough into the pan. Butter a 9-inch tart pan. Press the dough into the bottom and up the sides of the pan to form an even crust. Freeze for 1 hour.

3. Blind-bake. After the dough has chilled, preheat the oven to 375°F. Line the crust with parchment paper or foil and fill with pie weights or dried beans. Bake for 20 minutes. Remove the parchment paper and the weights. Prick the crust with a fork. Bake for 10 to 15 minutes more, or until golden brown. Let cool completely.

TO MAKE THE FILLING

1. Make the filling. In a medium bowl, using an electric mixer set on low and gradually increasing the speed to high, beat together the cream cheese, cream, powdered sugar, and vanilla for about 1 minute, or until stiff peaks form. Using a rubber spatula, fold in the melted white chocolate. Pour the filling into the crust and spread it in an even layer.

2. Top with the berries and chill. Top with the berries. Refrigerate for 3 hours before serving.

3. Serve. This tart is best served on the same day it is made. Serve at room temperature.

Summer Vegetable Tart

Makes 1 (9-inch) tart

When I bake, I love to use beautiful summer ingredients, like the fresh herbs and creamy goat cheese in this savory tart. *Nut-free*

PREP TIME: **45 minutes, plus 30 minutes to chill**
COOK TIME: **1 hour**

FOR THE CRUST

1 egg yolk, room temperature

2 tablespoons ice water

1¼ cups all-purpose flour

½ teaspoon salt

8 tablespoons (1 stick) unsalted butter, chilled and cut into cubes

TO MAKE THE CRUST

1. **Make the dough.** In a small bowl, mix together the egg yolk and water and set aside. In a large bowl, combine the flour and salt. Cut in the butter until the texture resembles coarse cornmeal. Add the egg mixture and mix with a fork until the dough begins to pull together.

2. **Refrigerate the dough.** Turn the dough out onto a sheet of plastic wrap and flatten it into a 4-inch disk. Tightly wrap it and refrigerate for 30 minutes.

3. **Roll out the dough.** Place the dough on a lightly floured work surface. Using a rolling pin, roll out the dough until it is about ⅛-inch thick.

4. **Shape the dough.** Butter a 9-inch tart pan. Transfer the dough to the pan. Trim the edges. Loosely wrap the pan in plastic wrap and chill for 30 minutes more.

5. **Blind-bake.** Preheat the oven to 375°F. Line the dough with parchment paper or foil. Fill with pie weights or dried beans. Bake 5 to 10 minutes, or until the edges begin to brown. Remove the parchment paper and the weights. Prick the crust with a fork. Bake for 5 minutes more, or until the bottom looks dry (and no longer raw). Lower the oven temperature to 350°F.

Continued ›

FOR THE FILLING

4 ounces goat cheese

1 teaspoon freshly
squeezed lemon juice

1 teaspoon garlic powder

Salt

Pepper

1 zucchini, cut into
¼-inch slices

1 yellow squash, cut into
¼-inch slices

1 tablespoon olive oil

1 tablespoon minced
fresh assorted herbs

TO MAKE THE FILLING AND ASSEMBLE THE TART

1. Make the filling. In a small bowl, mix together the goat cheese, lemon juice, and garlic. Season with salt and pepper.

2. Assemble the tart. Arrange the zucchini and squash between layers of paper towels and press down to absorb excess water. Spread the goat cheese mixture on the tart shell in an even layer. Arrange the zucchini and squash in an alternating pattern, slightly overlapping. Brush the vegetables with the oil. Sprinkle the herbs over the vegetables. Season with salt and pepper. Bake for 40 to 45 minutes, or until the vegetables are tender and cooked through.

SUBSTITUTION TIP: Add tomatoes, carrots, sweet potatoes, or eggplant to this tart for variety.

Bacon and Swiss Quiche

Makes 1 (9-inch) quiche

Though I've made different kinds of quiche,
I keep coming back to this classic. *Nut-free*

**PREP TIME: 10 minutes, plus
30 minutes to chill
COOK TIME: 1 hour 5 minutes,
plus 20 minutes to cool**

FOR THE CRUST
Basic Pie Dough
 (page 60)

FOR THE FILLING
5 large eggs, room
 temperature
½ cup whole milk
½ cup heavy cream
½ teaspoon salt
½ teaspoon pepper
8 bacon slices, cooked
 and chopped
1 shallot, diced
1½ cups shredded Swiss
 cheese, divided

TO MAKE THE CRUST

1. Roll out the dough. Place the pie dough on a lightly floured work surface. Using a rolling pin, roll out the dough into a 12-inch circle. Place the dough into a 9-inch pie dish. Leave a 1-inch overhang around the edge. Trim off any excess dough. Fold the overhang underneath itself around the edges, crimping as you go. Refrigerate for 30 minutes.

2. Blind-bake. Preheat the oven to 400°F. Line the dough with parchment paper or foil. Fill with pie weights or dried beans. Bake for about 15 minutes, or until the edges begin to brown. Remove the parchment and weights. Prick the crust with a fork. Bake for about 7 minutes more, or until the bottom crust is golden brown. Remove from the oven and allow to cool. Lower the oven temperature to 375°F.

TO MAKE THE FILLING AND ASSEMBLE THE QUICHE

1. Make the filling. In a large bowl, whisk together the eggs, milk, cream, salt, and pepper.

2. Assemble the quiche. Layer the bacon, shallot, and 1 cup of cheese on the bottom crust. Pour in the egg mixture. Top with the remaining ½ cup of cheese.

3. Bake. Bake for 40 to 45 minutes, or until the center is set. The quiche may bubble up but will flatten as it cools. Set on a wire rack to cool for 15 to 20 minutes.

SUBSTITUTION TIP: To make this vegetarian, substitute a 10-ounce frozen box of spinach, thawed and wrung free of water, for the bacon.

Mushroom Quiche

Makes 1 (9-inch) quiche

This hearty quiche full of mushrooms will be loved by
vegetarians and meat lovers alike. *Nut-free*

PREP TIME: **25 minutes, plus
30 minutes to chill**
COOK TIME:
**1 hour 15 minutes, plus
20 minutes to cool**

FOR THE CRUST

Basic Pie Dough
(page 60)

FOR THE FILLING

1 tablespoon oil

½ cup diced onion

3 cups sliced mushrooms

¼ cup diced red pepper

4 large eggs, room
temperature

½ cup milk

½ cup sour cream

½ teaspoon salt

½ teaspoon pepper

1½ cups shredded
Cheddar cheese,
divided

TO MAKE THE CRUST

1. Roll out the dough. Place the pie dough on a lightly
floured work surface. Using a rolling pin, roll out the
dough into a 12-inch circle. Place the dough into a
9-inch pie dish. Leave a 1-inch overhang around the
edge. Trim off any excess dough. Fold the overhang
underneath itself around the edge, crimping as you go.
Refrigerate for 30 minutes.

2. Blind-bake. Preheat the oven to 400°F. Line the
dough with parchment paper or foil. Fill with pie
weights or dried beans. Bake for about 15 minutes, or
until the edges begin to brown. Remove the parchment
and weights. Prick the crust with a fork. Bake for about
7 minutes more, or until the bottom crust is golden
brown. Remove from the oven and allow to cool. Lower
the oven temperature to 375°F.

TO MAKE THE FILLING AND ASSEMBLE THE QUICHE

1. Sauté the vegetables. In a large skillet, heat the oil
over medium heat. Add the onion, mushrooms, and red
pepper and sauté until cooked, 5 to 7 minutes.

2. Make the filling. In a medium bowl, whisk together
the eggs, milk, sour cream, salt, and pepper.

3. Assemble the quiche. Layer the mushroom mixture
and 1 cup of cheese on the bottom crust. Pour in the egg
mixture. Top with the remaining ½ cup of cheese.

4. Bake. Bake for 40 to 45 minutes, or until the center
is set. The quiche may bubble up but will flatten as it
cools. Set on a wire rack to cool for 15 to 20 minutes.

Sausage and Spinach Quiche

Makes 1 (9-inch) quiche

I usually make a bacon quiche, but one day I didn't have enough bacon, so I compromised and made a sausage quiche instead—it was a huge hit!

PREP TIME: **25 minutes, plus 30 minutes to chill**

COOK TIME: **1 hour 5 minutes, plus 20 minutes to cool**

FOR THE CRUST

Basic Pie Dough
(page 60)

FOR THE FILLING

5 large eggs, room
temperature

½ cup whole milk

½ cup heavy cream

½ teaspoon salt

½ teaspoon pepper

7 ounces sausage, cooked
and crumbled

1 cup spinach

1½ cups shredded
Cheddar cheese,
divided

1 shallot, diced

TO MAKE THE CRUST

1. **Roll out the dough.** Place the pie dough on a lightly floured work surface. Using a rolling pin, roll out the dough into a 12-inch circle. Place the dough into a 9-inch pie dish. Leave a 1-inch overhang around the edge. Trim off any excess dough. Fold the overhang underneath itself around the edge, crimping as you go. Refrigerate for 30 minutes.

2. **Blind-bake.** Preheat the oven to 400°F. Line the dough with parchment paper or foil. Fill with pie weights or dried beans. Bake until the edges are starting to brown, about 15 minutes. Remove the parchment paper and weights. Prick the crust with a fork. Bake for 7 minutes more, or until the bottom crust is beginning to brown and no longer looks raw. Remove from the oven and allow to cool on a wire rack. Lower the oven temperature to 375°F.

TO MAKE THE FILLING AND ASSEMBLE THE QUICHE

1. **Make the filling.** In a medium bowl, whisk together the eggs, milk, cream, salt, and pepper.

2. **Assemble the quiche.** Layer the sausage, spinach, 1 cup of cheese, and shallot on the bottom crust. Pour in the egg mixture. Top with the remaining ½ cup of cheese.

3. **Bake.** Bake for 40 to 45 minutes, or until the center is set. The quiche may bubble up but will flatten as it cools. Set on a wire rack to cool for 15 to 20 minutes.

SUBSTITUTION TIP: If you have vegetarians coming to brunch, swap out the sausage for mushrooms instead.

Blueberry Muffins PAGE 96

6

Can't-Fail Quick Breads and Masterful Muffins

Blueberry Muffins 96

Orange Muffins 97

Coffee Cake Muffins 98

Savory Cheddar and Herb Muffins 99

Zucchini Bread 100

Banana Bread 101

Coconut Bread 102

Strawberry Bread 103

Lemon and Poppy Seed Bread 104

Cranberry-Orange Bread 105

Cheesy Beer Bread 106

Honey Cornbread 107

Irish Soda Bread 108

Double Chocolate Chip Bread 109

Cinnamon Swirl Bread 110

Blueberry Muffins

Makes 12 muffins

These fluffy and moist muffins, bursting with sweet blueberries, will rival any bakery muffin. *Nut-free*

PREP TIME: 10 minutes
COOK TIME: 20 minutes

2¼ cups all-purpose flour

1 cup light brown sugar

1 tablespoon baking powder

¼ teaspoon salt

⅔ cup vegetable oil

½ cup plus 2 tablespoons milk

2 large eggs, room temperature

1½ teaspoons vanilla extract

2 cups blueberries, fresh or frozen

Coarse turbinado sugar, for sprinkling (optional)

1. **Preheat the oven.** Preheat the oven to 375°F. Lightly coat a muffin tin with cooking spray or line with paper liners.

2. **Combine the dry ingredients.** In a large bowl, combine the flour, brown sugar, baking powder, and salt. Make a well in the center of the flour mixture.

3. **Combine the wet ingredients.** In a medium bowl, whisk together the oil, milk, eggs, and vanilla.

4. **Add the wet ingredients.** Pour the wet ingredients into the well in the flour mixture. Using a rubber spatula, mix quickly and lightly. The batter will be lumpy. Stir in the blueberries. Fill each muffin cup about three-quarters full. Sprinkle with coarse sugar, if using.

5. **Bake.** Bake for 15 to 20 minutes, or until a toothpick inserted into the center comes out clean. Cool in the tin for 5 minutes. Transfer the muffins to a wire rack to cool completely.

SUBSTITUTION TIP: If you want to lighten these up and reduce the fat content, you could replace half of the oil with an equal amount of applesauce.

Orange Muffins

Makes 12 muffins

Bursting with fresh orange flavor, these sweet breakfast muffins
are a perfect way to jump-start your morning. *Nut-free*

PREP TIME: 10 minutes
COOK TIME: 15 minutes

2 cups all-purpose flour

1 tablespoon baking
powder

½ teaspoon salt

¾ cup granulated sugar

1 large egg, room
temperature

¾ cup milk

¼ cup orange juice

1 tablespoon grated
orange zest

¼ cup vegetable oil

1. **Preheat the oven.** Preheat the oven to 400°F. Lightly coat a muffin tin with cooking spray or line with paper liners.

2. **Combine the dry ingredients.** In a large bowl, combine the flour, baking powder, salt, and sugar. Make a well in the center of the flour mixture.

3. **Combine the wet ingredients.** In a medium bowl, whisk together the egg, milk, orange juice, orange zest, and oil.

4. **Add the wet ingredients.** Pour the wet ingredients into the well in the flour mixture. Using a rubber spatula, mix quickly and lightly. The batter will be lumpy. Fill each muffin cup about three-quarters full.

5. **Bake.** Bake for 15 minutes, or until a toothpick inserted into the center comes out clean. Cool in the tin for 5 minutes. Transfer the muffins to a wire rack to cool completely.

SUBSTITUTION TIP: Turn these into a citrus lover's dream by making the Powdered Sugar Glaze (page 170) and substituting orange juice for the milk.

Coffee Cake Muffins

Makes 12 muffins

To get through my lectures in college, I would always grab a giant coffee cake muffin at the little café near campus. This slightly smaller version is light and fluffy, spiced with cinnamon, and topped with a brown sugar crumb topping. *Nut-free*

PREP TIME: 10 minutes
COOK TIME: 20 minutes

FOR THE MUFFINS

2 cups all-purpose flour

¾ cup light brown sugar

½ teaspoon salt

1 teaspoon ground cinnamon

1 tablespoon baking powder

1 cup milk

½ cup vegetable oil

2 large eggs, room temperature

1 teaspoon vanilla extract

FOR THE TOPPING

⅔ cup all-purpose flour

⅓ cup light brown sugar

⅛ teaspoon salt

4 tablespoons (½ stick) unsalted butter, melted

1 teaspoon ground cinnamon

TO MAKE THE MUFFINS

1. **Preheat the oven.** Preheat the oven to 425°F. Lightly coat a muffin tin with cooking spray or line with paper liners.

2. **Combine the dry ingredients.** In a large bowl, whisk together the flour, sugar, salt, cinnamon, and baking powder. Make a well in the center of the flour mixture.

3. **Combine the wet ingredients.** In a medium bowl, whisk together the milk, oil, eggs, and vanilla.

4. **Add the wet ingredients.** Pour the wet ingredients into the well in the flour mixture. Using a rubber spatula, mix quickly and lightly. The batter will be lumpy. Fill each muffin cup about three-quarters full.

TO MAKE THE TOPPING

1. **Make the topping.** In a small bowl, combine all the topping ingredients and mix until crumbly. Sprinkle 1 tablespoon of topping over each muffin.

2. **Bake.** Bake for 15 to 20 minutes, or until a toothpick inserted into the center comes out clean. Cool in the tin for 5 minutes. Transfer the muffins to a wire rack to cool completely.

SUBSTITUTION TIP: Toss 1 cup of fresh blueberries or chocolate chips in 1 tablespoon of flour (so they don't sink and collect at the bottom) and fold them in after you add the wet ingredients to the dry ingredients.

Savory Cheddar and Herb Muffins

Makes 12 muffins

These cheesy muffins, made with chives and a hint of garlic, are a perfect accompaniment to a hearty bowl of soup or chili. *Nut-free*

PREP TIME: 10 minutes
COOK TIME: 20 minutes

2 cups all-purpose flour

1 teaspoon granulated sugar

2 teaspoons baking powder

2 teaspoons chopped fresh chives

1 cup shredded Cheddar cheese

1 teaspoon garlic powder

½ teaspoon salt

¾ cup buttermilk

8 tablespoons (1 stick) unsalted butter, melted and cooled

2 large eggs, room temperature

1. **Preheat the oven.** Preheat the oven to 350°F. Lightly coat a muffin tin with cooking spray or line with paper liners.

2. **Combine the dry ingredients.** In a large bowl, combine the flour, sugar, baking powder, chives, cheese, garlic powder, and salt. Make a well in the center of the flour mixture.

3. **Combine the wet ingredients.** In a medium bowl, whisk together the buttermilk, butter, and eggs.

4. **Add the wet ingredients.** Pour the wet ingredients into the well in the flour mixture. Using a rubber spatula, mix quickly and lightly. The batter will be lumpy. Fill each muffin cup about three-quarters full.

5. **Bake the muffins.** Bake for 20 minutes, or until a toothpick inserted into the center comes out clean. Cool in the tin for 5 minutes. Transfer the muffins to a wire rack to cool completely.

SUBSTITUTION TIP: Try using a different cheese, such as pepper jack, or try using chopped scallions instead of chives.

Zucchini Bread

Makes 1 (9-by-5-inch) loaf

One of the reasons I love summertime is because zucchini is abundant. Zucchini bread is an easy and delicious way to use it up. *Nut-free*

PREP TIME: 20 minutes
COOK TIME: 1 hour 5 minutes

3 cups all-purpose flour

1 teaspoon salt

1 teaspoon baking soda

1 teaspoon baking powder

1 tablespoon ground cinnamon

3 large eggs, room temperature

1 cup vegetable oil

1¼ cups granulated sugar

1 cup light brown sugar

1 tablespoon vanilla extract

3 cups shredded zucchini (about 3 medium zucchini)

1. **Preheat the oven.** Preheat the oven to 350°F. Butter a 9-by-5-inch loaf pan or lightly coat with cooking spray.

2. **Combine the dry ingredients.** In a medium bowl, combine the flour, salt, baking soda, baking powder, and cinnamon.

3. **Combine the wet ingredients.** In a large bowl, whisk together the eggs, oil, granulated sugar, brown sugar, and vanilla.

4. **Add the dry ingredients.** Add the dry ingredients to the wet ingredients and mix together with a rubber spatula until just combined. Fold in the zucchini.

5. **Bake.** Pour the batter into the pan and bake for 60 to 65 minutes, or until a toothpick inserted into the center comes out clean. Set the pan on a wire rack and cool completely.

SUBSTITUTION TIP: Stir in 1 cup of chocolate chips, toasted walnuts, or pecans tossed in 1 tablespoon of flour for a tasty addition to this bread.

Banana Bread

Makes 1 (9-by-5-inch) loaf

I love when my bananas start to overripen because that means it's time to make banana bread! This loaf is easy to make and has a hint of cinnamon.

PREP TIME: 15 minutes
COOK TIME: 1 hour

2½ cups all-purpose flour

1 teaspoon baking soda

1 teaspoon salt

¼ teaspoon ground cinnamon

1½ cups mashed very ripe bananas (3 to 4 medium bananas)

1¼ cups granulated sugar

½ cup vegetable oil

2 large eggs, room temperature

½ cup sour cream

1 teaspoon vanilla extract

1 cup toasted chopped walnuts (optional)

1. **Preheat the oven.** Preheat the oven to 350°F. Butter a 9-by-5-inch loaf pan or lightly coat with cooking spray.

2. **Combine the dry ingredients.** In a medium bowl, whisk together the flour, baking soda, salt, and cinnamon.

3. **Combine the wet ingredients.** In a large bowl, combine the banana, sugar, oil, eggs, sour cream, and vanilla.

4. **Add the dry ingredients.** Add the dry ingredients to the wet ingredients and mix together with a rubber spatula until just combined. Stir in the walnuts, if using.

5. **Bake.** Pour the batter into the pan and bake for 60 to 65 minutes, or until a toothpick inserted into the center comes out clean. Set the pan on a wire rack and cool completely.

SUBSTITUTION TIP: Instead of walnuts, try pecans or swap in indulgent chocolate chips!

Coconut Bread

Makes 1 (9-by-5-inch) loaf

I am a sucker for anything with coconut in it, and this
moist, tropical bread is no exception. *Nut-free*

PREP TIME: **20 minutes**
COOK TIME: **55 minutes**

2¼ cups all-purpose flour

1½ cups granulated sugar

¼ teaspoon salt

1 tablespoon baking
    powder

1½ cups canned coconut
    milk

3 large eggs, room
    temperature

6 tablespoons
    vegetable oil

1 teaspoon vanilla extract

2 teaspoons
    coconut extract

1 cup shredded
    sweetened coconut

1. **Preheat the oven.** Preheat oven to 350°F. Lightly
coat a 9-by-5-inch loaf pan with cooking spray.

2. **Combine the dry ingredients.** In a medium bowl,
combine the flour, sugar, salt, and baking powder.

3. **Combine the wet ingredients.** In a large bowl,
whisk together the coconut milk, eggs, oil, vanilla, and
coconut extract.

4. **Add the dry ingredients.** Add the dry ingredients
to the wet ingredients and mix together until just combined. Stir in the shredded coconut.

5. **Bake.** Pour the batter into the pan and bake for
50 to 55 minutes, or until a toothpick inserted into the
center comes out clean. Set the pan on a wire rack and
cool completely.

SUBSTITUTION TIP: Feel free to use regular milk instead
of coconut milk in this recipe. You can also substitute
unsweetened shredded coconut for the sweetened
shredded coconut.

Strawberry Bread

Makes 1 (8½-by-4½-inch) loaf

For a creative twist on strawberry shortcake, try topping this bread
with whipped cream and fresh sliced strawberries. *Nut-free*

PREP TIME: 20 minutes
COOK TIME: 1 hour 10 minutes

1½ cups all-purpose
flour, divided

1 cup granulated sugar

½ teaspoon salt

2 teaspoons baking
powder

¼ teaspoon ground
cinnamon

½ cup milk

¼ cup vegetable oil

2 large eggs, room
temperature

1 teaspoon vanilla extract

1½ cups diced
strawberries, tossed in
1 tablespoon flour

Granulated sugar, for
topping (optional)

1. **Preheat the oven.** Preheat the oven to 350°F. Butter
and flour an 8½-by-4½-inch loaf pan or lightly coat with
cooking spray.

2. **Combine the dry ingredients.** In a medium bowl,
whisk together the flour, sugar, salt, baking powder,
and cinnamon.

3. **Combine the wet ingredients.** In a large bowl, combine the milk, oil, eggs, and vanilla.

4. **Add the dry ingredients.** Add the dry ingredients
to the wet ingredients and mix together with a rubber
spatula until just combined. Stir in the strawberries.

5. **Bake.** Pour the batter into the pan and sprinkle with
sugar, if using. Bake for 60 to 70 minutes, or until a
toothpick inserted into the center comes out clean. Set
the pan on a wire rack and cool completely.

SUBSTITUTION TIP: Try using fresh raspberries instead
of strawberries.

Lemon and Poppy Seed Bread

Makes 1 (9-by-5-inch) loaf

This bread is great drizzled with a lemon glaze—just substitute lemon juice for the milk in the Powdered Sugar Glaze (page 170). *Nut-free*

PREP TIME: 20 minutes
COOK TIME: 55 minutes

2¼ cups all-purpose flour

1½ cups granulated sugar

½ teaspoon salt

1 tablespoon baking powder

1¼ cups sour cream

3 large eggs, room temperature

6 tablespoons vegetable oil

¼ cup freshly squeezed lemon juice

1 tablespoon grated lemon zest

2 teaspoons vanilla extract

3 tablespoons poppy seeds

1. **Preheat the oven.** Preheat the oven to 350°F. Butter and flour a 9-by-5-inch loaf pan or lightly coat with cooking spray.

2. **Combine the dry ingredients.** In a medium bowl, whisk together the flour, sugar, salt, and baking powder.

3. **Combine the wet ingredients.** In a large bowl, combine the sour cream, eggs, oil, lemon juice, lemon zest, and vanilla.

4. **Add the dry ingredients.** Add the dry ingredients to the wet ingredients and mix with a rubber spatula until just combined. Stir in the poppy seeds.

5. **Bake.** Pour the batter into the pan and bake for 60 to 65 minutes, or until a toothpick inserted into the center comes out clean. Set the pan on a wire rack and cool completely.

SUBSTITUTION TIP: For a different take, try substituting a different citrus, such as orange or lime, for the lemon.

Cranberry-Orange Bread

Makes 1 (9-by-5-inch) loaf

It's tough to resist the sweet and tart combination of cranberries and orange in this incredible bread. *Nut-free*

PREP TIME: 20 minutes
COOK TIME: 1 hour 5 minutes

2 cups all-purpose flour

½ teaspoon salt

½ teaspoon baking soda

½ teaspoon baking powder

3 large eggs, room temperature

½ cup vegetable oil

¾ cup granulated sugar

2½ teaspoons vanilla extract

¾ cup buttermilk

½ cup orange juice

1 tablespoon grated orange zest

1½ cups cranberries, tossed in 1 tablespoon flour

1. **Preheat the oven.** Preheat the oven to 350°F. Butter a 9-by-5-inch loaf pan or lightly coat with cooking spray.

2. **Combine the dry ingredients.** In a medium bowl, whisk together the flour, salt, baking soda, and baking powder.

3. **Combine the wet ingredients.** In a large bowl, combine the eggs, oil, sugar, vanilla, buttermilk, orange juice, and orange zest.

4. **Add the dry ingredients.** Add the dry ingredients to the wet ingredients and mix with a rubber spatula until just combined. Fold in the cranberries.

5. **Bake.** Pour the batter into the pan and bake for 60 to 65 minutes, or until a toothpick inserted into the center comes out clean. Set the pan on a wire rack and cool completely.

SUBSTITUTION TIP: If you can't find fresh cranberries, you can always use frozen cranberries instead. Do not thaw before stirring them into the batter.

Cheesy Beer Bread

Makes 1 (8½-by-4½-inch) loaf

Full of cheesy goodness, this is a quick, hearty, and
satisfying bread adults will love. *Nut-free*

PREP TIME: 20 minutes

COOK TIME: 50 minutes

2½ cups all-purpose flour

1 tablespoon baking
powder

1 teaspoon salt

⅛ teaspoon ground
pepper

1 cup shredded Cheddar
cheese

1 cup shredded
Parmesan cheese

1 cup beer

½ cup buttermilk

3 tablespoons unsalted
butter, melted and
slightly cooled

1 large egg, room
temperature

1. **Preheat the oven.** Preheat the oven to 350°F. Butter
and flour an 8½-by-4½-inch loaf pan or lightly coat with
cooking spray.

2. **Combine the dry ingredients.** In a medium bowl,
combine the flour, baking powder, salt, and pepper. Stir
in the Cheddar cheese and Parmesan cheese.

3. **Combine the wet ingredients.** In a large bowl,
whisk together the beer, buttermilk, butter, and egg
until combined.

4. **Add the dry ingredients.** Add the dry ingredients
to the wet ingredients and mix together with a rubber
spatula until just combined.

5. **Bake.** Pour the batter into the pan and bake for 45 to
50 minutes, or until a toothpick inserted into the center
comes out clean and the top is golden brown. Set the
pan on a wire rack and cool completely.

SUBSTITUTION TIP: If you prefer this without beer, you
can use plain seltzer water instead.

Honey Cornbread

Makes 1 (9-inch) round

I hold this moist cornbread recipe near and dear to my heart. Not only is it my grandmother's recipe, but I also entered it into my local 4-H fair as a kid and it won a blue ribbon. *Nut-free*

PREP TIME: 10 minutes
COOK TIME: 25 minutes

2 cups all-purpose flour

1½ cups yellow cornmeal

½ teaspoon salt

1 tablespoon baking powder

12 tablespoons (1½ sticks) unsalted butter

¼ cup granulated sugar

3 large eggs, room temperature

½ cup honey

1½ cups milk

1. **Preheat the oven.** Preheat the oven to 400°F. Butter a 9-inch round pan, square pan, or cast iron skillet.

2. **Combine the dry ingredients.** In a large bowl, whisk together the flour, cornmeal, salt, and baking powder.

3. **Cream the butter and sugar.** In a medium bowl, using an electric mixer, cream the butter and sugar until light and fluffy, about 2 minutes. Scrape down the bowl as needed.

4. **Add the remaining wet ingredients.** Add the eggs, one at a time, mixing well after each addition. Scrape down the bowl after each addition. Stir in the honey.

5. **Alternately add the dry ingredients and the milk.** Add the dry ingredients and the milk in alternating batches, beginning and ending with dry ingredients. Mix after each addition until just combined.

6. **Bake.** Pour the batter into the pan. Bake for 20 to 25 minutes, or until a toothpick inserted into the center comes out clean. Set the pan on a wire rack and cool completely.

SUBSTITUTION TIP: Try adding 1 cup of chopped cooked bacon, shredded Cheddar cheese, or diced jalapeño for a little kick.

Irish Soda Bread

Makes 1 (9-inch) round loaf

Adding a bit of sugar, raisins, and orange zest puts a
modern twist on classic Irish soda bread. *Nut-free*

PREP TIME: 15 minutes
COOK TIME: 50 minutes

4 cups all-purpose flour

4 tablespoons
granulated sugar

1 teaspoon baking soda

1 tablespoon baking
powder

½ teaspoon salt

8 tablespoons (1 stick)
unsalted butter,
room temperature and
cut into tablespoons

1 cup buttermilk

1 large egg, room
temperature

1 cup raisins

1 teaspoon grated
orange zest

1. Preheat the oven. Preheat the oven to 375°F.
Butter a 9-inch round cake pan or lightly coat with
cooking spray.

2. Make the dough. In a large bowl, using an electric mixer set on low, mix together the flour, sugar,
baking soda, baking powder, and salt. Add the butter,
1 tablespoon at a time, and continue mixing. Mix in the
buttermilk and egg.

3. Add the raisins and zest. Using a rubber spatula,
stir in the raisins and orange zest.

4. Shape the dough. Turn the dough into the pan and
shape it into a ball. Pat it down slightly into an 8- to
9-inch circle. Using a serrated knife, cut an "X" across
the top of the bread.

5. Bake. Bake for 45 to 50 minutes, or until the crust
is golden brown and the center appears baked through.
Set the pan on a wire rack and cool for 10 minutes.
Remove the bread from the pan, place it on the wire
rack, and cool completely.

SUBSTITUTION TIP: Instead of raisins, try currants, and
swap out the orange zest for caraway seeds.

Double Chocolate Chip Bread

Makes 1 (9-by-5-inch) loaf

You can enjoy this rich, fudgy bread any time of day, but I suggest serving it as a dessert alongside a cup of good, strong coffee. *Nut-free*

PREP TIME: 20 minutes
COOK TIME: 55 minutes

1½ cups all-purpose flour

½ cup unsweetened cocoa powder

½ teaspoon salt

½ teaspoon baking powder

½ teaspoon baking soda

½ cup vegetable oil

1 cup light brown sugar

2 large eggs, room temperature

1 cup buttermilk

1 cup semisweet chocolate chips, tossed with 1 tablespoon of flour

1. **Preheat the oven.** Preheat the oven to 350°F. Butter and flour a 9-by-5-inch loaf pan or lightly coat with cooking spray.

2. **Combine the dry ingredients.** In a medium bowl, whisk together the flour, cocoa powder, salt, baking powder, and baking soda.

3. **Combine the wet ingredients.** In a large bowl, combine the oil, sugar, eggs, and buttermilk.

4. **Add the dry ingredients.** Add the dry ingredients to the wet ingredients and mix together with a rubber spatula. Stir in the chocolate chips.

5. **Bake.** Pour the batter into the pan and bake for 50 to 55 minutes, or until a toothpick inserted into the center comes out clean. Set the pan on a wire rack and cool completely.

TOPPING TIP: Glaze the bread with Chocolate Ganache (page 171) and turn this into a triple chocolate bread!

Cinnamon Swirl Bread

Makes 1 (9-by-5-inch) loaf

I just can't resist anything that has a cinnamon swirl running through it, like this moist and comforting quick bread. *Nut-free*

PREP TIME: 20 minutes
COOK TIME: 55 minutes

FOR THE TOPPING

⅓ cup light brown sugar

2 teaspoons ground cinnamon

FOR THE BREAD

2 cups all-purpose flour

1 teaspoon baking soda

½ teaspoon salt

½ cup granulated sugar

½ cup light brown sugar

1 teaspoon vanilla extract

1 large egg, room temperature

1 cup buttermilk

¼ cup vegetable oil

TO MAKE THE TOPPING

Make the topping. In a small bowl, combine the brown sugar and cinnamon.

TO MAKE THE BREAD

1. **Preheat the oven.** Preheat the oven to 350°F. Butter and flour a 9-by-5-inch loaf pan or lightly coat with cooking spray.

2. **Combine the dry ingredients.** In a medium bowl, whisk together the flour, baking soda, and salt.

3. **Combine the wet ingredients.** In a second medium bowl, combine the granulated sugar, brown sugar, vanilla, egg, buttermilk, and oil.

4. **Combine wet and dry ingredients.** Add the dry ingredients to the wet ingredients and mix together with a rubber spatula.

5. **Make the swirl.** Pour half of the batter into pan. Sprinkle with half of the cinnamon and sugar mixture. Pour the remaining batter into the pan and top with the remaining cinnamon and sugar mixture. Draw a knife through batter, swirling in circles, to marble.

6. **Bake.** Pour the batter into the pan and bake for 50 to 55 minutes, or until a toothpick inserted into the center comes out clean. Set the pan on a wire rack and cool completely.

SUBSTITUTION TIP: If you don't have buttermilk, make your own. Combine 1 cup of milk with 1 tablespoon of lemon juice (or vinegar) and stir. Allow to sit for 10 minutes before using.

Red Velvet Layer Cake PAGE 134

Captivating Cakes
and Cupcakes

Vanilla Cupcakes 114

Chocolate Cupcakes 115

Lemon Cupcakes 116

Banana Cupcakes 117

Peanut Butter Cupcakes 118

Maple-Bacon Cupcakes 119

Snickerdoodle Cupcakes 120

Gingerbread Cake 121

Cinnamon Roll Cake 122

Carrot Sheet Cake 123

Pumpkin Cake 124

Orange Pound Cake 125

Chocolate Pudding Cake 126

Chocolate Zucchini Cake 127

Summer Peach Crumb Cake 128

Blueberry-Lemon Coffee Cake 129

Apple-Walnut Cake 130

Pineapple Upside-Down Cake 131

Vanilla Layer Cake 132

Chocolate Layer Cake 133

Red Velvet Layer Cake 134

Coconut Layer Cake 135

Hummingbird Layer Cake 136

Lemon-Raspberry Layer Cake 137

Vanilla Cupcakes

Makes 12 cupcakes

I've made these cupcakes countless times, including for my sister's wedding. They are easy to mix up and make the perfect canvas for any flavor of buttercream frosting. *Nut-free*

PREP TIME: **10 minutes**
COOK TIME: **22 minutes**

1½ cups all-purpose flour

1½ teaspoons baking powder

¼ teaspoon salt

8 tablespoons (1 stick) unsalted butter, melted and slightly cooled

1 cup granulated sugar

2 large eggs, room temperature

1 large egg white, room temperature

½ cup milk, room temperature

1 tablespoon vanilla extract

1. **Preheat the oven.** Preheat the oven to 350°F. Line a cupcake pan with paper liners.

2. **Combine the dry ingredients.** In a small bowl, combine the flour, baking powder, and salt.

3. **Combine the wet ingredients.** In a large bowl, whisk together the butter and sugar. Mix in the eggs and egg white until incorporated. Stir in the milk and vanilla.

4. **Add the dry ingredients.** Add the dry ingredients to the wet ingredients, mixing until just combined.

5. **Bake.** Fill each cupcake cup about two-thirds full. Bake for 18 to 22 minutes, or until a toothpick inserted into the center comes out clean. Cool in the pan for 5 minutes, then remove the cupcakes and place them on a wire rack to cool completely. Frost the cooled cupcakes as desired.

SUBSTITUTION TIP: For a colorful and festive version of this cupcake, stir ⅓ cup of sprinkles into the batter.

Chocolate Cupcakes

Makes 15 cupcakes

Every baker needs a great chocolate cupcake recipe in their arsenal for special occasions. These cupcakes are perfect with Vanilla or Chocolate Buttercream (page 176). *Nut-free*

PREP TIME: 10 minutes
COOK TIME: 14 minutes

- ¾ cup all-purpose flour
- ½ cup unsweetened cocoa powder
- 1¼ teaspoons baking powder
- ½ teaspoon baking soda
- ½ teaspoon salt
- 2 large eggs, room temperature
- ¾ cup granulated sugar
- 1½ teaspoons vanilla extract
- ½ cup vegetable oil
- ½ cup sour cream

1. **Preheat the oven.** Preheat the oven to 350°F. Line two cupcake pans with paper liners.

2. **Combine the dry ingredients.** In a small bowl, combine the flour, cocoa powder, baking powder, baking soda, and salt.

3. **Combine the wet ingredients.** In a large bowl, whisk together the eggs, sugar, vanilla, oil, and sour cream.

4. **Add the dry ingredients.** Add the dry ingredients to the wet ingredients, mixing until just combined.

5. **Bake.** Fill each cupcake cup about two-thirds full. Bake for 12 to 14 minutes, or until a toothpick inserted into the center comes out clean. Cool in the pan for 5 minutes, then remove the cupcakes and place them on a cooling rack to cool completely. Frost the cooled cupcakes as desired.

SUBSTITUTION TIP: If you don't have sour cream, you can use buttermilk or Greek yogurt instead.

Lemon Cupcakes

Makes 12 cupcakes

These fluffy cupcakes are bright and bursting with lemon flavor. They are perfect frosted with Cream Cheese Frosting (page 175). Or, for an even richer lemon flavor, use Vanilla Buttercream (page 176) with 3 tablespoons of freshly squeezed lemon juice stirred in. *Nut-free*

PREP TIME: 10 minutes
COOK TIME: 20 minutes

1¼ cups cake flour

1½ teaspoons baking powder

¼ teaspoon salt

6 tablespoons (¾ stick) unsalted butter, room temperature

¾ cup granulated sugar

1 large egg, room temperature

1 large egg white, room temperature

1 teaspoon vanilla extract

⅓ cup freshly squeezed lemon juice

1½ tablespoons grated lemon zest

½ cup milk

1. **Preheat the oven.** Preheat the oven to 350°F. Line a cupcake pan with paper liners.

2. **Combine the dry ingredients.** In a small bowl, whisk together the flour, baking powder, and salt.

3. **Cream the butter and sugar.** In a large bowl, using an electric mixer, cream the butter and sugar until light and fluffy, about 2 minutes.

4. **Add the remaining wet ingredients.** Add the egg and egg white, one at a time, mixing well after each addition, and then beat in the vanilla, lemon juice, and lemon zest.

5. **Alternately add the dry ingredients and the milk.** Add the dry ingredients and the milk to the butter mixture in alternating batches, beginning and ending with the dry ingredients. Mix after each addition until just combined. Scrape down the bowl as needed. After the last addition of flour, increase the mixer speed to medium-high. Mix just until no traces of flour remain, about 30 seconds. Do not overbeat.

6. **Bake.** Fill each cupcake cup about two-thirds full. Bake for 18 to 20 minutes, or until a toothpick inserted into the center comes out clean. Cool in the pan for 5 minutes, then remove the cupcakes and place them on a cooling rack to cool completely. Frost the cooled cupcakes as desired.

SUBSTITUTION TIP: Make these into lemon-blueberry cupcakes by stirring in ¾ cup of fresh or frozen blueberries.

Banana Cupcakes

Makes 16 cupcakes

If you like banana bread, you're going to love these light,
fluffy cinnamon-spiced cupcakes. *Nut-free*

PREP TIME: 10 minutes
COOK TIME: 20 minutes

1½ cups all-purpose flour

1½ teaspoons baking powder

½ teaspoon baking soda

¼ teaspoon salt

1 tablespoon ground cinnamon

1 cup granulated sugar

8 tablespoons (1 stick) unsalted butter, melted and slightly cooled

2 large eggs, room temperature

1 teaspoon vanilla extract

½ cup sour cream

½ cup mashed ripe bananas (2 to 3 medium bananas)

1. **Preheat the oven.** Preheat the oven to 350°F. Line two cupcake pans with paper liners.

2. **Combine the dry ingredients.** In a small bowl, combine the flour, baking powder, baking soda, salt, and cinnamon.

3. **Combine the wet ingredients.** In a large bowl, whisk together the sugar, butter, eggs, vanilla, sour cream, and bananas.

4. **Add the dry ingredients.** Add the dry ingredients to the wet ingredients, mixing until just combined.

5. **Bake.** Fill each cupcake cup about two-thirds full. Bake for 18 to 20 minutes, or until a toothpick inserted into the center comes out clean. Cool in the pan for 5 minutes, then remove the cupcakes and place them on a cooling rack to cool completely. Frost the cooled cupcakes as desired.

TOPPING TIP: I love frosting these with a peanut butter frosting, which can be made by stirring 1 cup of peanut butter into Vanilla Buttercream (page 176).

Peanut Butter Cupcakes

Makes 30 cupcakes

These cupcakes are especially fun when frosted with
Seven-Minute Icing (page 180), which brings a marshmallowy
twist reminiscent of a fluffernutter sandwich.

PREP TIME: **10 minutes**
COOK TIME: **20 minutes**

3 cups cake flour

1 tablespoon baking
powder

½ teaspoon salt

1 cup (2 sticks)
unsalted butter,
room temperature

2 cups granulated sugar

5 large eggs, room
temperature

2 tablespoons vanilla
extract

½ cup smooth peanut
butter

1¼ cups buttermilk

1. **Preheat the oven.** Preheat the oven to 350°F.
Line three cupcake pans with paper liners (or cook
in batches).

2. **Combine the dry ingredients.** In a large bowl,
whisk together the flour, baking powder, and salt.

3. **Cream the butter and sugar.** In a separate large
bowl, using an electric mixer, cream the butter and
sugar until light and fluffy, about 2 minutes.

4. **Add the remaining wet ingredients.** Add the eggs,
one at a time, mixing well after each addition, and then
beat in the vanilla and peanut butter.

5. **Alternately add the dry ingredients and the buttermilk.** Add the dry ingredients and the buttermilk to
the butter mixture in alternating batches, beginning
and ending with the dry ingredients. Mix after each
addition until just combined. Scrape down the bowl as
needed. After the last addition of flour, increase the
mixer speed to medium-high. Beat just until no traces
of flour remain, about 30 seconds. Do not overbeat.

6. **Bake.** Fill each cupcake cup about two-thirds full.
Bake for 18 to 20 minutes, or until a toothpick inserted
into the center comes out clean. Cool in the pan for
5 minutes, then remove the cupcakes and place them
on a cooling rack to cool completely. Frost the cooled
cupcakes as desired.

Maple-Bacon Cupcakes

Makes 18 cupcakes

These tender and moist cupcakes—made with brown sugar, maple syrup, and bacon—are the ultimate sweet and salty dessert or breakfast treat! *Nut-free*

PREP TIME: 15 minutes
COOK TIME: 22 minutes

2½ cups all-purpose flour

2 teaspoons baking powder

1 teaspoon baking soda

½ teaspoon salt

¾ teaspoon ground cinnamon

8 tablespoons (1 stick) unsalted butter, room temperature

½ cup light brown sugar

2 large eggs, room temperature

2 teaspoons vanilla extract

⅔ cup maple syrup

½ cup buttermilk

¾ cup crumbled cooked bacon, divided

1. **Preheat the oven.** Preheat the oven to 350°F. Line two cupcake pans with paper liners.

2. **Combine the dry ingredients.** In a medium bowl, whisk together the flour, baking powder, baking soda, salt, and cinnamon.

3. **Cream the butter and sugar.** In a large bowl, using an electric mixer, cream the butter and sugar until light and fluffy, about 2 minutes.

4. **Add the remaining wet ingredients.** Add the eggs, one at a time, mixing well after each addition. Mix in the vanilla and maple syrup.

5. **Alternately add the dry ingredients and the buttermilk.** Add the dry ingredients and the buttermilk to the butter mixture in alternating batches, beginning and ending with the dry ingredients. Mix after each addition until just combined. Using a rubber spatula, stir in ½ cup of bacon.

6. **Bake.** Fill each cupcake cup about two-thirds full. Bake for 18 to 22 minutes, or until a toothpick inserted into the center comes out clean. Cool in the pan for 5 minutes, then remove the cupcakes and place them on a cooling rack to cool completely. Frost the cooled cupcakes with your desired frosting and top each one with a sprinkle of the remaining ¼ cup of bacon.

TOPPING TIP: Make a maple buttercream frosting by stirring 1 teaspoon of maple extract or 3 tablespoons of maple syrup into Vanilla Buttercream (page 176).

Snickerdoodle Cupcakes

Makes 24 cupcakes

If you love snickerdoodle cookies, you'll swoon over these cupcakes. *Nut-free*

PREP TIME: **15 minutes**
COOK TIME: **22 minutes**

2½ cups all-purpose flour

2½ teaspoons baking powder

½ teaspoon baking soda

¼ teaspoon salt

2 teaspoons ground cinnamon

12 tablespoons (1½ sticks) unsalted butter, room temperature

½ cup granulated sugar

1 cup light brown sugar

2 large eggs, room temperature

2 teaspoons vanilla extract

1¼ cups buttermilk

1 tablespoon granulated sugar, for topping

1 teaspoon ground cinnamon, for topping

1. **Preheat the oven.** Preheat the oven to 375°F. Line two cupcake pans with paper liners.

2. **Combine the dry ingredients.** In a medium bowl, whisk together the flour, baking powder, baking soda, salt, and cinnamon.

3. **Cream the butter and sugars.** In a large bowl, using an electric mixer, cream the butter, granulated sugar, and brown sugar until light and fluffy, about 2 minutes.

4. **Add the remaining wet ingredients.** Add the eggs, one at a time, mixing well after each addition. Mix in the vanilla.

5. **Alternately add the dry ingredients and the buttermilk.** Add the dry ingredients and the buttermilk to the butter mixture in alternating batches, beginning and ending with the dry ingredients. Mix after each addition until just combined.

6. **Make the topping.** In a small bowl, combine the sugar and cinnamon for the topping. Sprinkle the topping over each cupcake before baking.

7. **Bake.** Fill each cupcake cup about two-thirds full. Bake for 18 to 22 minutes, or until a toothpick inserted into the center comes out clean. Cool in the pan for 5 minutes, then remove the cupcakes and place them on a cooling rack to cool completely. Frost the cooled cupcakes as desired.

TOPPING TIP: These are heavenly frosted with a cinnamon cream cheese frosting. Just add 1 tablespoon of cinnamon to Cream Cheese Frosting (page 175).

Gingerbread Cake

Makes 1 (9-inch) cake

Full of spices, molasses, and sweet honey, this gingerbread
cake is the perfect easy holiday-season dessert. Try it topped
with Stabilized Whipped Cream (page 179). *Nut-free*

PREP TIME: 15 minutes
COOK TIME: 35 minutes

2½ cups all-purpose flour

1½ teaspoons baking
soda

2 teaspoons ground
cinnamon

2 teaspoons ground
ginger

1 teaspoon ground cloves

½ teaspoon salt

½ cup dark brown sugar

½ cup vegetable oil

½ cup applesauce

1 large egg, room
temperature

½ cup molasses

½ cup honey

1 cup boiling water

1. **Preheat the oven.** Preheat the oven to 350°F. Lightly
coat a 9-inch round cake pan with cooking spray.

2. **Combine the dry ingredients.** In a medium bowl,
combine the flour, baking soda, cinnamon, ginger,
cloves, and salt.

3. **Combine the wet ingredients.** In a large bowl,
whisk together the sugar, oil, applesauce, egg, molasses,
and honey.

4. **Add the dry ingredients.** Add the dry ingredients to
the wet ingredients, mixing until just combined. Stir in
the boiling water.

5. **Bake.** Spread the batter in the pan in an even layer.
Bake for 30 to 35 minutes, or until a toothpick inserted
into the center comes out clean. Set the pan on a wire
rack and cool completely.

SUBSTITUTION TIP: If you don't have dark brown sugar,
substitute light brown sugar and add an extra
½ tablespoon of molasses.

Cinnamon Roll Cake

Makes 1 (9-by-13-inch) cake

This easy homemade vanilla cake batter has a sweet cinnamon sugar topping swirled through it. If you can't resist a big gooey cinnamon roll, then you are going to love this cake. *Nut-free*

PREP TIME: **15 minutes**
COOK TIME: **50 minutes**

FOR THE TOPPING

1 tablespoon ground cinnamon

1 cup light brown sugar

¼ teaspoon salt

FOR THE CAKE

3 cups all-purpose flour

2 teaspoons baking powder

½ teaspoon salt

1 cup granulated sugar

1 cup light brown sugar

1 cup (2 sticks) unsalted butter, melted and slightly cooled

4 large eggs, room temperature

2 teaspoons vanilla extract

1 cup milk

TO MAKE THE TOPPING

Make topping. In a small bowl, combine all the topping ingredients.

TO MAKE THE CAKE

1. Preheat the oven. Preheat the oven to 350°F. Lightly coat a 9-by-13-inch baking pan with cooking spray.

2. Combine the dry ingredients. In a medium bowl, combine the flour, baking powder, and salt.

3. Combine the wet ingredients. In a large bowl, whisk together the granulated sugar, brown sugar, butter, eggs, vanilla, and milk.

4. Add the dry ingredients. Add the dry ingredients to the wet ingredients, mixing until just combined.

5. Bake. Spread the batter in the pan in an even layer. Sprinkle the topping over the batter and swirl with a knife. Bake for 45 to 50 minutes until a toothpick inserted into the center comes out clean. Set the pan on a wire rack and cool completely. Frost the cooled cake as desired.

TOPPING TIP: I like to frost this cake with Powdered Sugar Glaze (page 170) or Cream Cheese Frosting (page 175).

Carrot Sheet Cake

Makes 1 (9-by-13-inch) cake

This perfectly spiced carrot sheet cake is easy to make, since the whole thing can be made in one bowl. I recommend grating the carrots by hand for the best texture and topping this cake with classic Cream Cheese Frosting (page 175). *Nut-free*

PREP TIME: 15 minutes
COOK TIME: 40 minutes

2 cups granulated sugar

½ cup vegetable oil

½ cup applesauce

4 large eggs, room temperature

2 cups all-purpose flour

½ teaspoon salt

1 teaspoon baking soda

1 teaspoon baking powder

2 teaspoons ground cinnamon

½ teaspoon ground nutmeg

½ teaspoon ground ginger

3 cups grated carrots (about 6 medium carrots)

1. **Preheat the oven.** Preheat the oven to 350°F. Lightly coat a 9-by-13-inch baking pan with cooking spray.

2. **Combine the wet ingredients.** In a large bowl, mix together the sugar, oil, applesauce, and eggs.

3. **Add the dry ingredients.** Add the flour, salt, baking soda, baking powder, cinnamon, nutmeg, and ginger. Stir to combine. Fold in the carrots.

4. **Bake.** Pour the batter into the pan. Bake for 35 to 40 minutes or until a toothpick inserted into the center comes out clean. Set the pan on a wire rack and cool completely. Frost the cooled cake as desired.

SUBSTITUTION TIP: For added crunch, fold in 1 cup of chopped, toasted pecans with the carrots in step 3.

Pumpkin Cake

Makes 1 (9-by-13-inch) cake

A moist spiced pumpkin cake that doesn't require an electric mixer and is ready to go in the oven in minutes? Sign me up! Finish this cake with a smooth layer of Cream Cheese Frosting (page 175). *Nut-free*

PREP TIME: **20 minutes**
COOK TIME: **35 minutes**

3 cups all-purpose flour

½ teaspoon salt

2 teaspoons baking soda

2 teaspoons ground cinnamon

¼ teaspoon ground nutmeg

¼ teaspoon ground cloves

½ teaspoon ground ginger

1 cup granulated sugar

1½ cups light brown sugar

1 cup vegetable oil

3 large eggs, room temperature

2 teaspoons vanilla extract

1 (15-ounce) can pumpkin purée

1. **Preheat the oven.** Preheat the oven to 350°F. Lightly coat a 9-by-13-inch baking pan with cooking spray.

2. **Combine the dry ingredients.** In a large bowl, whisk together the flour, salt, baking soda, cinnamon, nutmeg, cloves, and ginger.

3. **Combine the wet ingredients.** In a separate large bowl, whisk together the granulated sugar, brown sugar, oil, eggs, vanilla, and pumpkin purée until smooth and combined.

4. **Add the dry ingredients.** Add the dry ingredients to the wet ingredients, mixing until just combined.

5. **Bake.** Spread the batter in the pan in an even layer. Bake for 30 to 35 minutes, or until a toothpick inserted into the center comes out clean. Set the pan on a wire rack and cool completely. Frost the cooled cake as desired.

SUBSTITUTION TIP: If you're short on the individual spices, replace them with 1 tablespoon of pumpkin pie spice.

Orange Pound Cake

Makes 1 (10-inch) Bundt cake

When I first fell in love with baking, I enrolled in a class at a nearby culinary school. This bright, citrusy pound cake was one of the first recipes we learned to make. *Nut-free*

PREP TIME: 20 minutes
COOK TIME: 50 minutes

1 cup sour cream

1 teaspoon vanilla extract

2 tablespoons grated orange zest

2½ cups all-purpose flour

½ teaspoon baking powder

½ teaspoon baking soda

½ teaspoon salt

1 cup (2 sticks) unsalted butter, room temperature

2¼ cups granulated sugar

4 large eggs, room temperature

1. **Preheat the oven.** Preheat the oven to 350°F. Butter and flour a Bundt pan or two 9-by-5-inch loaf pans.

2. **Combine the wet ingredients.** In a small bowl, mix together the sour cream, vanilla, and orange zest.

3. **Sift the dry ingredients.** In a medium bowl, sift together the flour, baking powder, baking soda, and salt.

4. **Cream the butter and sugar.** In a large bowl, using an electric mixer, cream the butter and sugar until pale and fluffy, about 2 minutes.

5. **Add the eggs.** Add the eggs, one at a time, mixing well after each addition. Scrape down the bowl after each addition.

6. **Alternately add the dry ingredients and the sour cream mixture.** Add the dry ingredients and the sour cream mixture to the creamed butter and eggs in alternating batches, beginning and ending with the dry ingredients. Mix after each addition until just combined.

7. **Bake.** Spread the batter in the pan in an even layer. Bake for 50 minutes, or until a toothpick inserted into the center comes out clean. Cool in the pan for 10 minutes, then turn the cake out onto a wire rack and cool completely.

PREPARATION TIP: Make an orange glaze by adding 2 to 3 tablespoons of orange juice to Powdered Sugar Glaze (page 170). Pour the glaze over the top of the cake.

Chocolate Pudding Cake

Makes 1 (8-by-8-inch) cake

This quick, easy chocolate pudding cake forms a hot fudge layer underneath the cake as it bakes. Spoon some vanilla ice cream over it for an amazing sundae-style treat. *Nut-free*

PREP TIME: 10 minutes
COOK TIME: 25 minutes, plus 15 minutes to cool

FOR THE TOPPING

¼ cup light brown sugar

¼ cup granulated sugar

¼ cup unsweetened cocoa powder

1½ cups boiling water

FOR THE CAKE

1 cup all-purpose flour

1 cup granulated sugar

¼ cup unsweetened cocoa powder

2 teaspoons baking powder

½ teaspoon salt

½ cup milk

2 tablespoons vegetable oil

2 tablespoons butter

1½ teaspoons vanilla extract

TO MAKE THE TOPPING

Make the topping. In a small mixing bowl, combine the brown sugar, granulated sugar, and cocoa powder. Set aside.

TO MAKE THE CAKE

1. Preheat the oven. Preheat the oven to 350°F. Butter an 8-by-8-inch baking pan or coat it lightly with cooking spray.

2. Combine the dry ingredients. In a small bowl, combine the flour, sugar, cocoa powder, baking powder, and salt.

3. Combine the wet ingredients. In a large bowl, whisk together the milk, oil, butter, and vanilla.

4. Add the dry ingredients. Add the dry ingredients to the wet ingredients and mix until just combined.

5. Bake. Spread the batter in the pan in an even layer. Sprinkle the topping over the batter. Pour the boiling water over the topping. Do not stir. Bake for about 25 minutes, or until the top is set. Cool in the pan for about 15 minutes. Serve the cake warm, spooning it into bowls and drizzling a generous amount of the sauce over the cake.

SUBSTITUTION TIP: If you love dark chocolate, substitute dark cocoa powder for the regular unsweetened cocoa powder. It will yield a richer, darker, and more bittersweet chocolate cake.

Chocolate Zucchini Cake

Makes 1 (9-by-13-inch) cake

In the summertime, I always seem to have way too much zucchini
on my hands. This wonderful, fudgy cake is great way to use it up.
Try it with Chocolate Buttercream (page 176). *Nut-free*

PREP TIME: 15 minutes
COOK TIME: 1 hour

2 cups all-purpose flour

2¼ cups granulated sugar

¾ cup unsweetened
cocoa powder

2 teaspoons baking soda

1 teaspoon baking
powder

½ teaspoon salt

1 teaspoon vanilla extract

4 large eggs, room
temperature

1 cup vegetable oil

3 cups grated zucchini

¾ cup semisweet
chocolate chips

1. **Preheat the oven.** Preheat the oven to 350°F. Lightly
coat a 9-by-13-inch baking pan with cooking spray.

2. **Combine the dry ingredients.** In a medium bowl,
combine the flour, sugar, cocoa powder, baking soda,
baking powder, and salt.

3. **Combine the wet ingredients.** In a large
bowl, whisk together the vanilla, eggs, and oil
until combined.

4. **Add the dry ingredients.** Add the dry ingredients to
the wet ingredients and mix until just combined. Stir in
the zucchini and chocolate chips.

5. **Bake.** Spread the batter in the pan in an even layer.
Bake for 50 minutes to 1 hour, or until a toothpick
inserted into the center comes out clean. Set the pan on
a wire rack and cool completely. Frost the cooled cake
as desired.

TROUBLESHOOTING TIP: The key to this moist cake
is to not wring out the zucchini, ensuring it retains
its moisture.

Summer Peach Crumb Cake

Makes 1 (9-inch) cake

This simple, fresh peach cake is the perfect summery treat!
Easy to make and topped with juicy ripe peaches, this cake
will quickly become a summertime favorite. *Nut-free*

PREP TIME: **20 minutes**

COOK TIME: **1 hour 10 minutes**

FOR THE TOPPING

1½ cups all-purpose flour

2 teaspoons ground cinnamon

12 tablespoons (1½ sticks) unsalted butter, melted

½ cup light brown sugar

½ teaspoon salt

FOR THE CAKE

1½ cups all-purpose flour

1½ teaspoons baking powder

½ teaspoon salt

6 tablespoons (¾ stick) unsalted butter, room temperature

1 cup granulated sugar

1 large egg, room temperature

½ cup milk

1 teaspoon vanilla extract

1 pound peaches, peeled and sliced (2 to 3 peaches)

TO MAKE THE TOPPING

Make the topping. In a small bowl, mix together all the topping ingredients until crumbly.

TO MAKE THE CAKE

1. Preheat the oven. Preheat the oven to 350°F. Lightly coat a 9-inch round cake pan with cooking spray.

2. Combine the dry ingredients. In a small bowl, whisk together the flour, baking powder, and salt.

3. Cream the butter and sugar. In a large bowl, using an electric mixer, cream the butter and sugar until light and fluffy, about 2 minutes.

4. Add the remaining wet ingredients. Mix in the egg, milk, and vanilla until just combined.

5. Add the dry ingredients. Add the dry ingredients to the wet ingredients, mixing until just combined.

6. Bake. Spread the batter in the pan in an even layer. Top with the peaches. Sprinkle the topping over the batter in an even layer. Bake for 10 minutes, then reduce the oven temperature to 325°F and bake until golden brown and a toothpick inserted into the center comes out clean, 50 minutes to 1 hour. Set the pan on a wire rack and cool completely.

SUBSTITUTION TIP: Substitute another fresh fruit such as plums, cherries, or strawberries for the peaches.

Blueberry-Lemon Coffee Cake

Makes 1 (9-by-13-inch) cake

Bursting with blueberries, lemon zest, and Greek yogurt, this cake is crowned with a crunchy cinnamon crumble. *Nut-free*

PREP TIME: 20 minutes
COOK TIME: 1 hour

FOR THE TOPPING

1 cup light brown sugar

½ cup granulated sugar

1½ tablespoons ground cinnamon

½ teaspoon salt

1 cup (2 sticks) unsalted butter, melted and slightly cooled

2½ cups all-purpose flour

FOR THE CAKE

2½ cups all-purpose flour

1 teaspoon baking soda

¾ teaspoon baking powder

½ teaspoon salt

12 tablespoons (1½ sticks) unsalted butter, room temperature

1½ cups granulated sugar

2 large eggs, room temperature

1½ teaspoons vanilla extract

1¼ cups Greek yogurt

1 tablespoon grated lemon zest

2 cups blueberries (fresh or frozen)

TO MAKE THE TOPPING

Make the topping. In a small bowl, whisk together the brown sugar, granulated sugar, cinnamon, and salt. Stir in the melted butter. Add the flour and stir with a fork until moist clumps form.

TO MAKE THE CAKE

1. **Preheat the oven.** Preheat the oven to 350°F. Lightly coat a 9-by-13-inch baking pan with cooking spray.

2. **Combine the dry ingredients.** In a medium bowl, whisk together the flour, baking soda, baking powder, and salt.

3. **Cream the butter and sugar.** In a large bowl, using an electric mixer, cream the butter and sugar until light and fluffy, about 2 minutes.

4. **Add the remaining wet ingredients.** Add the eggs, one at a time, mixing well after each addition. Scrape down the bowl as needed. Stir in the vanilla, yogurt, and lemon zest.

5. **Add the dry ingredients.** Add one-third of the dry ingredients and mix until just incorporated. Repeat two times to use up all the flour. Fold in the blueberries.

6. **Bake.** Spread the batter in the pan in an even layer. Sprinkle the topping over the batter. Bake for 1 hour, or until a toothpick inserted into the center comes out clean and the topping is a deep golden brown and slightly crisp. Set the pan on a wire rack and let cool completely.

TOPPING TIP: Drizzle with Powdered Sugar Glaze (page 170).

Apple-Walnut Cake

Makes 1 (9-inch) cake

This moist snack cake spiced with cinnamon, sweet apples,
and walnuts doesn't even need a frosting; simply dust with
a touch of powdered sugar and amaze your guests.

PREP TIME: 20 minutes
COOK TIME: 45 minutes

8 tablespoons (1 stick)
   unsalted butter,
   room temperature

½ cup granulated sugar

½ cup light brown sugar

2 large eggs, room
   temperature

1 teaspoon vanilla extract

1¼ cups all-purpose flour

1 teaspoon baking soda

2 teaspoons ground
   cinnamon

½ teaspoon salt

1½ cups shredded apple

½ cup toasted chopped
   walnuts or pecans

1. **Preheat the oven.** Preheat the oven to 350°F. Butter
and flour a 9-inch round cake pan.

2. **Cream the butter and sugars.** In large bowl, using
an electric mixer, cream the butter, granulated sugar,
and brown sugar until light and fluffy, about 2 minutes.

3. **Add the remaining ingredients.** Add the eggs, one
at a time, mixing well after each addition. Stir in the
vanilla, flour, baking soda, cinnamon, and salt. Stir in
the apples and walnuts.

4. **Bake.** Spread the batter in the pan in an even layer.
Bake for 40 to 45 minutes, or until a toothpick inserted
into the center comes out clean. Cool in the pan for
10 minutes, then turn the cake out onto a wire rack and
cool completely.

SUBSTITUTION TIP: For more spice and flavor, swap out
the cinnamon and use apple pie spice instead.

Pineapple Upside-Down Cake

Makes 1 (9-inch) cake

Baking a cake upside down is a technique that dates to when baking was done in cast iron skillets. This modern version yields a buttery cake topped with mouthwatering caramelized pineapple. *Nut-free*

PREP TIME: **20 minutes**

COOK TIME: **50 minutes**

FOR THE TOPPING

1 (20-ounce) can pineapple slices

4 tablespoons (½ stick) unsalted butter, melted

⅔ cup light brown sugar

14 maraschino cherries

FOR THE CAKE

1½ cups all-purpose flour

1½ teaspoons baking powder

¼ teaspoon baking soda

¼ teaspoon salt

½ cup (1 stick) unsalted butter, room temperature

1 cup granulated sugar

2 large eggs, room temperature

2½ teaspoons vanilla extract

⅔ cup buttermilk

TO MAKE THE TOPPING

1. **Preheat the oven.** Preheat the oven to 350°F. Lightly coat a 9-inch round cake pan with cooking spray.

2. **Make the topping**. Drain the pineapple. In the 9-inch round pan, mix together the butter and sugar. Place the pineapple slices in the sugar mixture (8 on the bottom and cut the remaining 3 slices in half and place around the sides of the pan). Place a cherry in the center of each pineapple slice, in the center of the pan, and around the sides.

TO MAKE THE CAKE

1. **Combine the dry ingredients.** In a small bowl, combine the flour, baking powder, baking soda, and salt.

2. **Cream the butter and sugar.** In a large bowl, using an electric mixer, cream the butter and sugar until light and fluffy, about 2 minutes. Add the eggs, one at a time, mixing well after each addition. Mix in the vanilla.

3. **Alternately add the dry ingredients and the buttermilk.** Add the dry ingredients and the buttermilk to the creamed butter in alternating batches, beginning and ending with dry ingredients. Mix after each addition until just combined.

4. **Bake.** Bake for 45 to 50 minutes, or until a toothpick inserted into the center comes out clean. Cool in the pan for 5 minutes. Loosen the edges, place a serving platter over the pan, and invert the cake onto the platter.

Vanilla Layer Cake

Makes 1 (9-inch) cake

Every baker needs a great vanilla cake recipe in their arsenal. This is a great option, and a wonderful blank canvas for myriad fillings and frostings, including Vanilla or Chocolate Buttercream (page 176) or Berry Buttercream (page 178). *Nut-free*

PREP TIME: **20 minutes**
COOK TIME: **35 minutes**

3¼ cups cake flour

1 tablespoon baking powder

1 teaspoon salt

8 tablespoons (1 stick) unsalted butter, room temperature

½ cup vegetable oil

2 cups granulated sugar

4 large eggs, room temperature

1 tablespoon vanilla extract

1½ cups buttermilk

1. **Preheat the oven.** Preheat the oven to 350°F. Butter and flour two 9-inch round cake pans.

2. **Combine the dry ingredients.** In a large bowl, whisk together the flour, baking powder, and salt.

3. **Cream the butter and sugar.** In a separate large bowl, using an electric mixer, cream the butter, oil, and sugar until light and fluffy, about 2 minutes.

4. **Add the eggs and vanilla.** Add the eggs, one at a time, mixing well after each addition. Scrape down the bowl after each addition. Mix in the vanilla.

5. **Alternately add the dry ingredients and the buttermilk.** Add the dry ingredients and the buttermilk to the creamed butter in alternating batches, beginning and ending with the dry ingredients. Mix after each addition until just combined.

6. **Bake.** Pour half of the batter into each pan. Bake for 30 to 35 minutes, or until golden brown around the edges and a toothpick inserted into the center comes out clean. Cool in the pans for 5 minutes, then turn the cakes out onto a wire rack to cool completely. Frost the cooled cake first between the layers, then on the top, and then around the sides.

PREPARATION TIP: Try adding fruit curd, preserves, or even sliced strawberries between the layers.

Chocolate Layer Cake

Makes 1 (9-inch) cake

Perfect for every birthday table's centerpiece, this cake is light, made in just one bowl, and brimming with sweetness. Besting any boxed option, this one's for the kids (and the kids-at-heart). Go all in on the chocolate and frost this with Chocolate Buttercream (page 176). *Nut-free*

PREP TIME: 20 minutes
COOK TIME: 35 minutes

2¼ cups all-purpose flour

2 teaspoons baking soda

¾ cup unsweetened cocoa powder

½ teaspoon salt

½ cup vegetable oil

1 cup light brown sugar

1 cup granulated sugar

3 large eggs, room temperature

1½ teaspoons vanilla extract

1 cup buttermilk

1 cup boiling water

1. **Preheat the oven.** Preheat the oven to 350°F. Butter and flour two 9-inch round cake pans.

2. **Combine the dry ingredients.** In a large bowl, whisk together the flour, baking soda, cocoa powder, and salt.

3. **Combine the wet ingredients.** In a medium bowl, whisk together the oil, brown sugar, granulated sugar, eggs, vanilla, and buttermilk until smooth.

4. **Combine the wet and dry ingredients.** Pour the wet mixture into the flour mixture and whisk to combine. Stir in the boiling water.

5. **Bake.** Pour half of the batter into each pan. Bake for 30 to 35 minutes, or until a toothpick inserted into the center comes out clean. Cool in the pans for 5 minutes, then turn the cakes out onto a wire rack to cool completely. Frost the cooled cake first between the layers and then on the top and around the sides.

SUBSTITUTION TIP: For a mocha flavor, add 1 teaspoon of espresso powder to the boiling water.

Red Velvet Layer Cake

Makes 1 (9-inch) cake

This iconic showstopper has a slight buttermilk tang and a hint of chocolate, making this cake perfect for Valentine's Day, Christmas, or any festive occasion. *Nut-free*

PREP TIME: 20 minutes
COOK TIME: 35 minutes

2½ cups cake flour

1½ teaspoons baking soda

3 tablespoons unsweetened cocoa powder

1 teaspoon salt

½ cup vegetable oil

1½ cups granulated sugar

2 large eggs, room temperature

2 tablespoons red food coloring

1½ teaspoons vanilla extract

1 cup buttermilk

1 tablespoon distilled white vinegar

1. **Preheat the oven.** Preheat the oven to 350°F. Butter and flour two 9-inch round cake pans.

2. **Combine the dry ingredients.** In a large bowl, whisk together the flour, baking soda, cocoa powder, and salt.

3. **Combine the wet ingredients.** In a medium bowl, mix the oil, sugar, eggs, food coloring, vanilla, buttermilk, and vinegar until smooth.

4. **Combine the wet and dry ingredients.** Pour the wet mixture into flour mixture and, using a rubber spatula, stir to combine.

5. **Bake.** Pour half of the batter into each pan. Bake for 30 to 35 minutes, or until a toothpick inserted into the center comes out clean. Cool in the pans for 5 minutes, then turn the cakes out onto a wire rack to cool completely. Frost the cooled cake first between the layers and then on the top and around the sides.

PREPARATION TIP: A classic frosting pairing is, of course, Cream Cheese Frosting (page 175). Or try Fluffy White (Boiled Milk) Icing (page 174) for something a bit different.

Coconut Layer Cake

Makes 1 (9-inch) cake

Packed full of tender, sweet coconut, this moist cake is a
coconut lover's dream. Coconut Buttercream (page 177)
adds the perfect finishing touch. *Nut-free*

PREP TIME: 30 minutes
COOK TIME: 26 to 30 minutes

1 cup canned coconut
milk

4 tablespoons (½ stick)
unsalted butter,
melted

⅓ cup vegetable oil

2 cups cake flour

2 teaspoons baking
powder

1¼ teaspoons salt

4 large eggs, room
temperature

2 cups granulated sugar

1 teaspoon vanilla extract

2 teaspoons coconut
extract

1 cup shredded
sweetened coconut

1. **Preheat the oven.** Preheat the oven to 325°F. Butter
and flour two 9-inch cake pans.

2. **Combine the wet ingredients.** In a small bowl, mix
together the coconut milk, butter, and oil.

3. **Sift the dry ingredients.** In a separate small bowl,
sift together the flour, baking powder, and salt.

4. **Mix the eggs and sugar.** In a large bowl, using
an electric mixer with a whisk attachment set on
medium-high, beat the eggs, sugar, vanilla, and coconut
extract until thickened and light gold in color, about
2 minutes. The batter should fall in thick ribbons from
the whisk.

5. **Alternately add the dry ingredients and the
coconut milk mixture.** Add the dry ingredients and
the coconut milk mixture to the eggs and sugar in
alternating batches, beginning and ending with the
dry ingredients. Mix after each addition until just combined. Stir in the shredded coconut.

6. **Bake.** Pour half of the batter into each pan. Bake
until a toothpick inserted into the center comes out
clean and the top feels set, 26 to 30 minutes. Cool in
the pans for 10 minutes, then turn the cakes out onto
a wire rack and cool completely. Frost the cooled cake
first between the layers and then on the top and around
the sides.

SUBSTITUTION TIP: If you can't find canned coconut
milk, replace it with whole milk.

Hummingbird Layer Cake

Makes 1 (9-inch) cake

This Southern favorite is chock-full of spices, bananas, pecans, and pineapple and is typically frosted with Cream Cheese Frosting (page 175).

PREP TIME: 20 minutes
COOK TIME: 30 minutes

3 cups all-purpose flour

1 cup granulated sugar

1 cup light brown sugar

1 teaspoon baking soda

1½ teaspoons ground cinnamon

½ teaspoon ground allspice

1 teaspoon salt

1½ cups vegetable oil

3 large eggs, room temperature

1 (8-ounce) can crushed pineapple, drained

2 cups mashed bananas (5 to 6 bananas)

1½ teaspoons vanilla extract

1 cup chopped pecans

1. **Preheat the oven.** Preheat the oven to 350°F. Butter and flour two 9-inch round cake pans.

2. **Sift the dry ingredients.** In a large bowl, sift together the flour, granulated sugar, brown sugar, baking soda, cinnamon, allspice, and salt.

3. **Combine the wet ingredients.** In a separate large bowl, combine the oil, eggs, pineapple, bananas, vanilla, and pecans.

4. **Add the dry ingredients.** Add the dry ingredients to the wet ingredients, mixing until just combined.

5. **Bake.** Pour half of the batter into each pan. Bake for 25 to 30 minutes, or until a toothpick inserted into the center comes out clean. Cool in the pans for 5 minutes, then loosen the edges and turn the cakes out onto a wire rack to cool completely. Frost the cooled cake first between the layers and then on the top and around the sides.

SUBSTITUTION TIP: You can substitute ¼ teaspoon of cinnamon, ¼ teaspoon of cloves, and a pinch of ground nutmeg for the allspice.

Lemon-Raspberry Layer Cake

Makes 1 (9-inch) cake

Sweet raspberries and tart lemon play wonderfully off each
other in this light and fluffy cake, making it the perfect
treat for a Mother's Day or Easter brunch. *Nut-free*

PREP TIME: 20 minutes
COOK TIME: 30 minutes

2¾ cups all-purpose flour

1⅔ cups granulated sugar

1 tablespoon baking
    powder

½ teaspoon baking soda

¾ teaspoon salt

12 tablespoons (1½ sticks)
    unsalted butter,
    room temperature

1 tablespoon grated
    lemon zest

4 large egg whites, room
    temperature

1 large egg, room
    temperature

1 cup milk

1½ teaspoons vanilla
    extract

⅓ cup freshly squeezed
    lemon juice

1½ cups fresh raspberries

1. **Preheat the oven.** Preheat the oven to 350°F. Butter
and flour two 9-inch round cake pans.

2. **Combine the dry ingredients and butter.** In a large
bowl, using an electric mixer set on low, mix together
the flour, sugar, baking powder, baking soda, and
salt. Add the butter and mix until crumbly. Add the
lemon zest.

3. **Add the eggs.** Add the egg whites, one at a time,
then the whole egg, beating well after each addition.
Scrape down the bowl after each addition.

4. **Add the remaining ingredients.** In a small bowl,
whisk together the milk, vanilla, and lemon juice. Add
this mixture, one-third at a time, to the batter. Beat for
1 to 2 minutes after each addition, until fluffy. Scrape
down the bowl as needed. Fold in the raspberries.

5. **Bake.** Pour half of the batter into each pan. Bake for
25 to 30 minutes, or until a toothpick inserted into the
center comes out clean. Cool in the pans for 10 minutes,
then turn the cakes out onto a wire rack to cool completely. Frost the cooled cake first between the layers
and then on the top and around the sides.

SUBSTITUTION TIP: You can also use frozen raspberries. To mix up the fruity element, try blueberries instead
of raspberries. To finish, try Cream Cheese Frosting
(page 175) with 2 tablespoons of freshly squeezed lemon
juice added in.

Jalapeño-Cheddar Biscuits **PAGE 151**

8

Beautiful Breads, Biscuits, and Crackers

Buttery Round Crackers 140

Whole-Wheat Crackers 142

Homemade Cheddar
Cheese Crackers 143

Olive Oil Flatbread Crackers 144

Saltine Crackers 145

Graham Crackers 146

Spicy Chili Crackers 147

Garlic-Parmesan Crackers 148

Buttermilk Biscuits 149

Whole-Wheat Biscuits 150

Jalapeño-Cheddar Biscuits 151

Shortcake Biscuits 152

Apple-Cinnamon Scones 153

Maple-Bacon Scones 154

Sweet Hawaiian Rolls 155

Orange Sweet Rolls 156

Cinnamon Swirl Bread 158

No-Knead Cranberry-Pecan
Bread 160

Basic French Bread 162

White Sandwich Bread 163

Braided Challah 164

Knotted Herb-Garlic
Dinner Rolls 166

Buttery Round Crackers

Makes 5 to 6 dozen

This classic cracker recipe brings me back to my childhood and that
time-tested pairing of chicken soup and crispy crackers. *Nut-free*

PREP TIME: 30 minutes
COOK TIME: 25 minutes

2 cups all-purpose flour

1 tablespoon baking
powder

1 teaspoon granulated
sugar

½ teaspoon salt

8 tablespoons (1 stick)
unsalted butter, chilled
and cut into cubes

⅔ cup milk

1 large egg, beaten, for
the egg wash

1 tablespoon water, for
the egg wash

Salt, for topping

1. Preheat the oven. Position a rack in the middle of
the oven. Preheat the oven to 400°F. Line two baking
sheets with parchment paper or silicone baking mats.

2. Combine the dry ingredients. In a large bowl, using
an electric mixer set on low, combine the flour, baking
powder, sugar, and salt.

3. Cut in the butter. Cut in the butter, a few small
tablespoons at a time, until the texture resembles
coarse crumbs.

4. Add the milk. Add the milk a little bit at a time.
The dough should start to form a ball. Divide the dough
in half and work in batches. Wrap the half you are not
working with in plastic wrap and refrigerate it.

5. Roll out the dough. Place the dough on a lightly
floured surface and knead it a few times until it comes
together in a smooth ball. Roll out the dough as thin as
possible, adding more flour to your work surface if the
dough begins to stick.

6. **Cut the crackers.** Using a 2-inch round cookie cutter, cut out the crackers and place them on the baking sheets. Gather up and reroll the scraps as thinly as possible, then cut out more crackers. Repeat until all the dough is used up. Using a fork, prick each cracker a few times.

7. **Make the egg wash.** Beat the egg and water together until well combined. Brush the crackers with the egg wash, then sprinkle the salt over them.

8. **Bake.** Bake for 10 to 12 minutes on the middle rack until golden brown and no longer soft to the touch. Cool on the baking sheets for 5 minutes. Transfer the crackers to a wire rack to cool completely. Repeat steps 5 through 8 with the second batch of dough.

PREPARATION TIP: Bring a new level of flavor to these crackers by adding 1 tablespoon of fresh herbs or seeds, such as rosemary, dill, or sesame seeds.

Whole-Wheat Crackers

Makes 8 dozen

Made with butter and milk, these crackers are rich and full
of flavor. Perfectly crispy and crunchy, they also taste great
with herbs or cheeses mixed into the dough. *Nut-free*

PREP TIME: 15 minutes
COOK TIME: 15 minutes

1½ cups all-purpose flour

1½ cups whole-wheat
flour

1 teaspoon granulated
sugar

2 teaspoons salt

4 tablespoons (½ stick)
unsalted butter,
melted

1 cup milk

1 large egg, beaten, for
the egg wash

1 tablespoon water, for
the egg wash

Coarse sea salt, for
sprinkling

1. **Preheat the oven.** Preheat the oven to 375°F. Line
two baking sheets with parchment paper or silicone
baking mats.

2. **Make the dough.** In a large bowl, using a rubber
spatula, combine the all-purpose flour, whole-wheat
flour, sugar, and salt. Add the butter and milk and stir
until a sticky dough forms. Divide the dough in half and
work in batches.

3. **Roll out the dough.** Place the dough on a lightly
floured work surface. Using a rolling pin, roll out the
dough to a ⅛-inch thickness.

4. **Cut the crackers**. Using a pizza cutter or sharp
knife, cut the dough into 1-inch-wide strips. Then cut
crosswise to make rectangles. Using a fork, prick each
cracker a few times. Place the crackers on the baking
sheets. (Crackers will not spread, so they can be close
together, just not touching.)

5. **Make the egg wash.** Beat the egg and water together
until well combined. Brush the crackers with the egg
wash, then sprinkle the salt over them.

6. **Bake.** Bake for about 15 minutes, or until the
crackers are browned and crisp. Transfer the crackers
to a wire rack to cool completely.

SUBSTITUTION TIP: To lighten these up further, swap
water for the milk and use oil instead of the butter.

Homemade Cheddar Cheese Crackers

Makes 6 to 7 dozen

This homemade version of those classic, square cheesy crackers is incredibly simple to make. *Nut-free*

PREP TIME: 15 minutes, plus 30 minutes to chill

COOK TIME: 15 minutes

2 tablespoons unsalted butter, room temperature

1 cup shredded sharp Cheddar cheese

¼ teaspoon salt

½ cup all-purpose flour

1 to 2 tablespoons cold water

1. **Preheat the oven.** Preheat the oven to 375°F. Line two baking sheets with parchment paper or silicone baking mats.

2. **Combine the butter, cheese, and salt.** In a medium bowl, using a rubber spatula, combine the butter, cheese, and salt.

3. **Add the flour and water.** Using a fork, mix the flour into the cheese mixture until crumbly. Sprinkle in the cold water. Using a rubber spatula, mix the dough until it comes together and holds its shape when pressed together.

4. **Refrigerate the dough.** Turn the dough out onto a sheet of plastic wrap. Press it into a thick disk and wrap it tightly. Refrigerate for 30 minutes.

5. **Roll out the dough.** Place the dough on a lightly floured work surface. Using a rolling pin, roll out the dough to a ⅛-inch thickness.

6. **Cut the crackers.** Using a pizza cutter or sharp knife, cut the dough into 1-inch-wide strips. Then cut crosswise to make rectangles. Using a fork, prick each cracker a few times. Place the crackers on the baking sheets.

7. **Bake.** Bake for about 15 minutes, or until the crackers are browned and crisp. Transfer the crackers to a wire rack to cool completely.

SUBSTITUTION TIP: Try another type of hard cheese, such as Parmesan.

Olive Oil Flatbread Crackers

Makes 6 to 7 dozen

If you're seeking a simple cracker recipe to serve with a dip, look no further. Be sure to roll the dough very thin so you get crunchy crackers. *Dairy-free, Nut-free*

PREP TIME: **30 minutes**
COOK TIME: **30 minutes**

1½ cups all-purpose flour

1 teaspoon salt

1 teaspoon granulated sugar

½ teaspoon freshly ground black pepper

3 tablespoons olive oil, plus more for topping

½ cup cold water

Coarse sea salt, for topping

1. **Preheat the oven.** Preheat the oven to 400°F. Line two baking sheets with parchment paper or silicone baking mats.

2. **Make the dough.** In a medium bowl, combine the flour, salt, sugar, and pepper. Drizzle with the oil and add the water. Using a fork, mix the oil and water into the flour mixture until it comes together in a sticky dough and pulls away from the sides of the bowl.

3. **Knead the dough.** Place the dough on a lightly floured surface and knead the dough. Add flour as necessary. Knead until the dough no longer sticks to work surface. Divide the dough in half and work in batches.

4. **Roll out the dough.** Lightly flour a clean work surface. Using a rolling pin, roll out the dough to a ⅛-inch thickness.

5. **Cut the crackers.** Using a pizza cutter or sharp knife, cut the dough into 1-inch-wide strips. Then cut crosswise to make rectangles. Using a fork, prick each cracker a few times. Place the crackers on the baking sheets. Brush the crackers with oil, then sprinkle the salt over them.

6. **Bake.** Bake for 10 to 15 minutes, or until the crackers are browned and crisp. Transfer the crackers to a wire rack to cool completely. Repeat steps 4 through 6 with the second batch of dough.

PREPARATION TIP: Try sprinkling sesame seeds over the crackers with the sea salt in step 5 for an added nutty crunch.

Saltine Crackers

Makes 4 dozen

With a little butter and salt in each crispy bite, these crackers come together easily and use common pantry staples. *Nut-free*

PREP TIME: 1 hour
COOK TIME: 1 hour

4 cups all-purpose flour

1 tablespoon baking powder

1 teaspoon salt

2 tablespoons unsalted butter, melted

2 tablespoons oil (vegetable, canola, or olive)

⅔ cup water

1 large egg, beaten, for the egg wash

1 tablespoon of water, for the egg wash

Coarse sea salt, for topping

1. **Preheat the oven.** Preheat the oven to 400°F. Line two baking sheets with parchment paper or silicone baking mats.

2. **Make the dough.** In a large bowl, using a rubber spatula, combine the flour, baking powder, and salt. Stir in the butter and oil. Add the water gradually until it forms a sticky dough. Divide the dough into 4 portions and work in batches.

3. **Roll out the dough.** Place the dough on a lightly floured work surface. Using a rolling pin, roll out the dough to a ⅛-inch thickness.

4. **Cut the crackers.** Using a pizza cutter or sharp knife, cut the dough into 1-inch-wide strips. Then cut crosswise to make rectangles. Using a fork, prick each cracker a few times. Place the crackers on the baking sheet.

5. **Make the egg wash.** Beat the egg and water together until well combined. Brush the crackers with the egg wash, then sprinkle the salt over them.

6. **Bake.** Bake for 12 to 15 minutes, or until the crackers are browned and crisp. Transfer the crackers to a wire rack to cool completely. Repeat steps 3 through 6 with each batch of dough.

PREPARATION TIP: Try adding ½ teaspoon of fresh ground pepper, 1 tablespoon of chopped fresh herbs, or ¼ cup of shredded cheese to the dough.

Graham Crackers

Makes 4 dozen

Made with whole-wheat flour, cinnamon, and brown sugar, these crackers are slightly sweet and crispy. All they need is a toasted marshmallow and chocolate square to complete them. *Nut-free*

PREP TIME: 40 minutes, plus 30 minutes to chill
COOK TIME: 40 minutes

2 cups all-purpose flour

½ cup whole-wheat flour

½ teaspoon ground cinnamon

¼ teaspoon baking soda

½ teaspoon salt

8 tablespoons (1 stick) unsalted butter, room temperature

¼ cup granulated sugar

½ cup light brown sugar

¼ cup water

Coarse turbinado sugar, for sprinkling

1. **Combine the dry ingredients.** In a medium bowl, combine the all-purpose flour, whole-wheat flour, cinnamon, baking soda, and salt.

2. **Cream the butter and sugars.** In a large bowl, using an electric mixer, cream the butter, granulated sugar, and brown sugar until light and fluffy, about 2 minutes.

3. **Add the flour and water.** With the mixer set on low, add one-third of the flour mixture and 2 tablespoons of water. Mix for 30 seconds. Add one-third of the flour, and the remaining 2 tablespoons of the water. Then add the remaining flour and mix until just combined.

4. **Knead the dough.** Place the dough on a lightly floured surface and knead it for about 10 seconds. Divide the dough in half and work in batches. Cover the second batch of dough with plastic wrap.

5. **Roll out the dough.** Using a rolling pin, roll out the dough to a ⅛-inch thickness.

6. **Cut the crackers.** Using a pizza cutter or sharp knife, cut the dough into 1-inch-wide strips. Then cut crosswise to make rectangles. Using a fork, prick each cracker a few times. Arrange the crackers on two baking sheets lined with parchment paper or silicone baking mats. Sprinkle each cracker with the coarse sugar. Cover with plastic wrap and refrigerate for 30 minutes.

7. **Bake.** About 15 minutes before you are ready to bake the crackers, preheat the oven to 350°F. Bake for 15 to 20 minutes, or until the edges are a dark golden color. Cool on the baking sheets for 10 minutes. Transfer the crackers to a wire rack to cool completely. Repeat steps 5 through 7 with the second batch of dough.

Spicy Chili Crackers

Makes 8 dozen

With chili powder, red pepper flakes, and hot sauce in the mix, these crackers—my husband's favorite—pack a punch. *Dairy-free, Nut-free*

PREP TIME: **30 minutes**
COOK TIME: **30 minutes**

3 cups all-purpose flour

1 teaspoon granulated sugar

1 teaspoon chili powder

½ teaspoon cumin

½ teaspoon red pepper flakes

2 teaspoons salt

4 tablespoons olive oil, plus more for topping

1 cup water

½ teaspoon hot sauce

Sea salt, for topping

1. **Preheat the oven.** Preheat the oven to 375°F. Line two baking sheets with parchment paper or silicone baking mats.

2. **Make the dough.** In a large bowl, using a rubber spatula, combine the flour, sugar, chili powder, cumin, red pepper flakes, and salt. Stir in the oil, water, and hot sauce and mix until a sticky dough forms. Divide the dough in half and work in batches.

3. **Roll out the dough.** Place the dough on a lightly floured work surface. Using a rolling pin, roll out the dough to a ⅛-inch thickness.

4. **Cut the crackers.** Using a pizza cutter or sharp knife, cut the dough into 1-inch-wide strips. Then cut crosswise to make rectangles. Using a fork, prick each cracker a few times. Place the crackers on the baking sheets. Brush the crackers with the oil, then sprinkle the salt over them.

5. **Bake.** Bake for 15 minutes, or until the crackers are browned and crisp. Cool on the baking sheets for 10 minutes. Transfer the crackers to a wire rack to cool completely. Repeat steps 3 through 5 with the second batch of dough.

SUBSTITUTION TIP: If you don't have hot sauce on hand, try adding sriracha instead.

Garlic-Parmesan Crackers

Makes 8 dozen

These easy-to-make crackers pair perfectly with a veggie
dip for effortless entertaining. *Nut-free*

PREP TIME: 30 minutes
COOK TIME: 30 minutes

1½ cups all-purpose flour

½ cup freshly grated
   Parmesan cheese

1 teaspoon granulated
   sugar

1 tablespoon garlic
   powder

½ teaspoon salt

3 tablespoons olive oil,
   plus more for topping

½ cup cold water

Sea salt, for topping

1. **Preheat the oven.** Preheat the oven to 375°F. Line two baking sheets with parchment paper or silicone baking mats.

2. **Make the dough.** In a medium bowl, using a rubber spatula, combine the flour, Parmesan cheese, sugar, garlic powder, and salt. Stir in the oil and water and mix until a sticky dough forms. Divide the dough in half and work in batches.

3. **Roll out the dough.** Place the dough on a lightly floured work surface. Using a rolling pin, roll out the dough to a ⅛-inch thickness.

4. **Cut the crackers.** Using a pizza cutter or sharp knife, cut the dough into 1-inch-wide strips. Then cut crosswise to make rectangles. Using a fork, prick each cracker a few times. Place the crackers on the baking sheets. Brush the crackers with oil, then sprinkle salt over them.

5. **Bake.** Bake for 15 minutes until the crackers are browned and crisp. Cool on the baking sheets for 5 minutes. Transfer the crackers to a wire rack to cool completely. Repeat steps 3 through 5 with the second batch of dough.

SUBSTITUTION TIP: Substitute another cheese—such as Colby, Swiss, or Cheddar—for the Parmesan.

Buttermilk Biscuits

Makes 10 to 12 biscuits

These flaky, tender biscuits take less than 30 minutes to throw together and are the perfect treat to make on a lazy weekend. *Nut-free*

PREP TIME: 10 minutes
COOK TIME: 15 minutes

3 cups all-purpose flour

4 teaspoons baking powder

½ teaspoon baking soda

½ teaspoon salt

8 tablespoons (1 stick) unsalted butter, chilled and cut into cubes

1 cup cold buttermilk, plus more for topping

Butter, melted, for topping

1. **Preheat the oven.** Preheat the oven to 425°F. Line a baking sheet with parchment paper or a silicone baking mat.

2. **Sift the dry ingredients.** In a large bowl, sift together the flour, baking powder, baking soda, and salt.

3. **Cut in the butter.** Cut in the butter until the butter is in pea-size pieces. Pour in the buttermilk and stir to combine.

4. **Shape and cut the biscuits.** Place the dough onto a lightly floured work surface. Pat the dough into a ½-inch-thick circle and fold the dough in half. Pat out the dough again and fold it in half. Repeat 2 to 3 times. Using a 2½-inch biscuit cutter or the rim of a large drinking glass, press straight down into the dough. Do not twist the cutter, which can cause biscuits to come out lopsided. Cut out as many biscuits as you can from the first circle, then gather up the scraps and reshape into a ½-inch-thick circle (try to handle the dough as little as possible) and cut out the remaining biscuits.

5. **Bake.** Place the biscuits next to each other on the baking sheet so they touch. Brush them with buttermilk. Bake for 15 minutes, or until lightly golden brown on top. When they come out of the oven, brush the tops of the biscuits with the melted butter. Serve immediately.

SUBSTITUTION TIP: You can transform these biscuits by stirring in 1 cup fresh blueberries along with the buttermilk.

Whole-Wheat Biscuits

Makes 10 to 12 biscuits

These hearty, flaky biscuits are easy to make and the perfect vehicle for a breakfast sandwich or just eaten solo!

PREP TIME: 10 minutes
COOK TIME: 15 minutes

1¼ cups all-purpose flour

1 cup whole-wheat flour

1 tablespoon baking powder

1 teaspoon salt

6 tablespoons unsalted butter, chilled and cut into cubes

¾ cup buttermilk, plus more for topping

1 tablespoon honey

Butter, melted, for topping

1. **Preheat the oven.** Preheat the oven to 425°F. Line a baking sheet with parchment paper or a silicone baking mat.

2. **Combine the dry ingredients.** In a medium bowl, whisk together the all-purpose flour, whole-wheat flour, baking powder, and salt.

3. **Cut in the butter.** Cut in the butter until the butter is in pea-size pieces. Pour in the buttermilk and honey and stir to combine.

4. **Shape and cut the biscuits.** Place the dough onto a lightly floured work surface. Pat the dough into a ½-inch-thick circle and fold the dough in half. Pat out the dough again and fold it in half. Repeat 2 to 3 times. Using a 2½-inch biscuit cutter or the rim of a large drinking glass, press straight down into the dough. Do not twist the cutter, which can cause biscuits to come out lopsided. Cut out as many biscuits as you can from the first circle, then gather up the scraps and reshape into a ½-inch-thick circle (try to handle the dough as little as possible) and cut out the remaining biscuits.

5. **Bake the biscuits.** Place the biscuits next to each other on the baking sheet so they touch. Brush them with buttermilk. Bake for 15 minutes, or until lightly golden brown on top. When they come out of the oven, brush the tops of the biscuits with the melted butter. Serve immediately.

SUBSTITUTION TIP: You can substitute all or part of the flour with white whole-wheat flour.

Jalapeño-Cheddar Biscuits

Makes 10 to 12 biscuits

These buttermilk biscuits, with gooey cheese and bits of jalapeño, are the perfect spicy accompaniment to a hearty bowl of soup or chili. *Nut-free*

PREP TIME: 10 minutes
COOK TIME: 10 minutes

2 cups all-purpose flour

1 tablespoon baking powder

½ teaspoon baking soda

½ teaspoon salt

8 tablespoons (1 stick) unsalted butter, chilled and cut into cubes

1 cup shredded Cheddar cheese

1 jalapeño, diced

¾ cup cold buttermilk, plus more for topping

Butter, melted, for topping

1. **Preheat the oven.** Preheat the oven to 450°F. Line a baking sheet with parchment paper or a silicone baking mat.

2. **Combine the dry ingredients.** In a medium bowl, whisk together the flour, baking powder, baking soda, and salt.

3. **Cut in the butter.** Cut in the butter until the butter is in pea-size pieces. Stir in the cheese and jalapeño. Pour in the buttermilk and stir.

4. **Shape and cut the biscuits.** Place the dough onto a lightly floured work surface. Pat the dough into a ½-inch-thick circle and fold the dough in half. Pat out the dough again and fold it in half. Repeat 2 to 3 times. Using a 2½-inch biscuit cutter or the rim of a large drinking glass, press straight down into the dough. Do not twist the cutter, which can cause biscuits to come out lopsided. Cut out as many biscuits as you can from the first circle, then gather up the scraps and reshape into a ½-inch-thick circle (try to handle the dough as little as possible) and cut out the remaining biscuits.

5. **Bake.** Place the biscuits next to each other on the baking sheet so they touch. Brush them with the buttermilk. Bake for 10 minutes, until golden brown. When they come out of the oven, brush the tops of the biscuits with the melted butter. Serve immediately.

SUBSTITUTION TIP: If you want less heat, remove the ribs and seeds from the jalapeño before chopping. Or swap out the pepper for 1 tablespoon of chives instead!

Shortcake Biscuits

Makes 10 to 12 biscuits

I grew up eating strawberry shortcake on bland store-bought biscuits, but now I like to serve that classic dessert on these homemade sweet, buttery biscuits instead. *Nut-free*

PREP TIME: 10 minutes
COOK TIME: 15 minutes

2 cups all-purpose flour

¼ cup granulated sugar, plus more for topping

1 tablespoon baking powder

¾ teaspoon salt

4 tablespoons (½ stick) unsalted butter, chilled and cut into cubes

1 cup cold heavy cream, plus more for topping

1. **Preheat the oven.** Preheat the oven to 425°F. Line a baking sheet with parchment paper or a silicone baking mat.

2. **Combine the dry ingredients.** In a medium bowl, whisk together the flour, sugar, baking powder, and salt.

3. **Cut in the butter.** Cut in the butter until the butter is in pea-size pieces. Stir in the cream.

4. **Shape and cut the biscuits.** Place the dough onto a lightly floured work surface. Pat the dough into a ½-inch-thick circle and fold the dough in half. Pat out the dough again and fold it in half. Repeat 2 to 3 times. Using a 2½-inch biscuit cutter or the rim of a large drinking glass, press straight down into the dough. Do not twist the cutter, which can cause biscuits to come out lopsided. Cut out as many biscuits as you can from the first circle, then gather up the scraps and reshape into a ½-inch-thick circle (try to handle the dough as little as possible) and cut out the remaining biscuits.

5. **Bake.** Place the biscuits next to each other on the baking sheet so they touch. Brush them with the cream and sprinkle the sugar over the tops. Bake for 12 to 15 minutes, or until the tops are golden brown. Cool on a wire rack.

SUBSTITUTION TIP: If you don't have heavy cream, you can substitute buttermilk or regular milk.

Apple-Cinnamon Scones

Makes 8 scones

These moist, tender cinnamon scones loaded with fresh apples
will make your kitchen smell amazing. *Nut-free*

PREP TIME: 10 minutes
COOK TIME: 22 minutes

2¾ cups all-purpose flour

⅓ cup granulated sugar

¾ teaspoon salt

1 tablespoon baking
   powder

2 teaspoons ground
   cinnamon

¼ teaspoon ground
   nutmeg

¼ teaspoon ground
   cloves

8 tablespoons (1 stick)
   unsalted butter, chilled
   and cut into cubes

¾ cup chopped fresh
   apple

½ cup cold heavy cream

2 large eggs, room
   temperature

1 teaspoon vanilla extract

1. **Preheat the oven.** Preheat the oven to 425°F. Line a baking sheet with parchment paper or a silicone baking mat.

2. **Combine the dry ingredients.** In a large bowl, whisk together the flour, sugar, salt, baking powder, cinnamon, nutmeg, and cloves.

3. **Cut in the butter.** Cut in the butter until the butter is in pea-size pieces. Using a rubber spatula, stir in the apple.

4. **Combine the wet ingredients**. In a glass measuring cup (or small bowl), mix together the cream, eggs, and vanilla. Pour the cream mixture into the flour mixture and stir.

5. **Shape and cut the scones.** Place the dough onto a lightly floured work surface. Pat the dough into a ½-inch-thick circle and fold the dough in half. Pat out the dough again and fold it in half. Repeat 2 to 3 times. Pat the dough into an 8-inch circle. Using a sharp knife cut the circle into 8 triangle wedges. Place the scones on a baking sheet about 2 inches apart.

6. **Bake.** Bake for 18 to 22 minutes, or until golden brown. Transfer to a wire rack to cool completely.

PREPARATION TIP: I love drizzling these scones with an apple cider glaze. Simply make the Powdered Sugar Glaze (page 170) and substitute apple cider for the milk.

Maple-Bacon Scones

Makes 8 scones

These scones have the perfect combination of salty and
sweet that you look for in a breakfast treat. *Nut-free*

PREP TIME: **10 minutes**
COOK TIME: **25 minutes**

3 cups all-purpose flour

¾ teaspoon salt

1 tablespoon baking
powder

8 tablespoons (1 stick)
unsalted butter, chilled
and cut into cubes

1 cup bacon, crumbled
and cooked

⅓ cup maple syrup

2 large eggs

½ cup cold milk

1. **Preheat the oven.** Preheat the oven to 425°F. Line
a baking sheet with parchment paper or a silicone
baking mat.

2. **Combine the dry ingredients.** In a large bowl,
whisk together the flour, salt, and baking powder.

3. **Cut in the butter.** Cut in the butter until the butter
is in pea-size pieces. Using a rubber spatula, stir in
the bacon.

4. **Combine the wet ingredients.** In a small bowl, mix
together the maple syrup, eggs, and milk. Stir the milk
mixture into the flour mixture.

5. **Shape and cut the scones.** Place the dough onto
a lightly floured work surface. Pat the dough into a
½-inch-thick circle and fold the dough in half. Pat out
the dough again and fold it in half. Repeat 2 to 3 times.
Pat the dough into an 8-inch circle. Using a sharp knife,
cut the circle into 8 triangle wedges. Place the scones on
a baking sheet about 2 inches apart.

6. **Bake.** Bake for 20 to 25 minutes. Transfer to a wire
rack to cool completely.

SUBSTITUTION TIP: Take these over the edge by drizzling a maple syrup glaze over them. Simply add ¼ cup of
maple syrup to the Powdered Sugar Glaze (page 170).

Sweet Hawaiian Rolls

Makes 15 rolls

Sweetened with pineapple juice and brown sugar, these pillowy
soft dinner rolls are easier to make than you think! *Nut-free*

**PREP TIME: 30 minutes, plus
1 hour 30 minutes to rise
COOK TIME: 15 minutes**

⅔ cup whole milk,
    warmed to 105°F
    to 110°F

⅔ cup pineapple juice,
    room temperature

¼ cup light brown sugar

3 tablespoons unsalted
    butter, melted

1 teaspoon salt

2¼ teaspoons instant
    yeast

4 cups bread flour

1 large egg, room
    temperature

1 egg yolk, room
    temperature

Butter, melted, for
    topping

1. **Make the dough.** In a large bowl, using a wooden
spoon or in the bowl of a stand mixer using a paddle
attachment, combine the milk, pineapple juice, sugar,
melted butter, salt, yeast, flour, egg, and egg yolk.

2. **Knead the dough.** Place the dough on a lightly
floured surface and knead for about 10 minutes. If
using a stand mixer, attach the dough hook and knead
on medium-high for 4 to 5 minutes. When a soft and
smooth ball of dough forms, place the dough in a large,
lightly greased bowl, and turn once to coat. Cover the
bowl with a clean dish towel or plastic wrap and allow
the dough to rise until doubled in size, about 1 hour.

3. **Preheat the oven.** Preheat the oven to 375°F.
Butter a 9-by-13-inch baking pan or lightly coat with
cooking spray.

4. **Shape the rolls.** Punch down the dough, then
place it on a lightly floured work surface. Flatten the
dough into a 12-by-8-inch rectangle. Cut the dough
into 5 strips and then cut each strip into 3 equal portions. Roll each portion into a ball and place it in the
pan. Cover the pans with greased plastic wrap, and let
the rolls rise for 30 minutes, or until doubled in size
and puffy.

5. **Bake.** Bake for 15 minutes, or until golden brown.
Brush the rolls with butter before serving.

SUBSTITUTION TIP: You can use all-purpose flour
instead of bread flour, though the texture of the rolls
might be slightly different.

Orange Sweet Rolls

Makes 12 rolls

These fluffy sweet rolls are flavored with orange juice and zest and ready in just about an hour, making them the perfect treat for a Mother's Day brunch. *Nut-free*

PREP TIME: **20 minutes, plus 25 minutes to rise**
COOK TIME: **20 minutes**

FOR THE DOUGH

½ cup whole milk, warmed to 105°F to 110°F

½ cup orange juice

⅓ cup (5⅓ tablespoons) unsalted butter

½ cup granulated sugar

1 teaspoon salt

4 to 4½ cups all-purpose flour, divided

2¼ teaspoons rapid rise (fast-acting) yeast

1 tablespoon grated orange zest

1 large egg, room temperature

FOR THE FILLING

1 cup light brown sugar

2 tablespoons ground cinnamon

⅓ cup (5⅓ tablespoons) unsalted butter, room temperature

TO MAKE THE DOUGH

1. **Combine the milk, juice, butter, sugar, and salt.** In a small saucepan over medium heat, heat the milk, orange juice, butter, sugar, and salt until the butter is melted, then remove from the heat and let cool.

2. **Add the flour.** In a large bowl, using a wooden spoon or a stand mixer fitted with a dough hook attachment, combine 2 cups of flour, the yeast, and orange zest.

3. **Add the butter mixture.** Add the cooled butter mixture into the flour mixture and mix. Stir in the egg.

4. **Add the remaining flour.** Add the remaining 2 cups of flour. Scrape the edges of the bowl and make sure the flour is fully incorporated.

5. **Knead the dough.** Place the dough on a lightly floured work surface and knead for 10 minutes (or on low for 5 minutes in a stand mixer). If the dough seems overly sticky (you want it to be a little bit sticky), stir in 2 tablespoons of flour at a time until it starts pulling away from the bowl. Let the dough rest for 5 minutes.

6. **Prepare the pan.** Lightly butter a 9-by-13-inch baking pan or coat it lightly with cooking spray.

7. **Shape the rolls.** Lightly flour your work surface and roll the dough into a 12-by-16-inch rectangle.

1. Make the filling. In a small bowl, mix together the sugar and cinnamon.

2. Add the filling. Spread the softened butter all the way to the edge of both short sides and one long side of the dough. On the remaining long side, leave a 1-inch strip of dough. Sprinkle the cinnamon sugar evenly over the butter, leaving the 1-inch border uncovered. Lightly press the cinnamon sugar into the butter. Tightly roll the dough up into a log, starting on the long end that has the filling right to the edge and finishing with the plain dough on the bottom, where you will seal the entire thing together. Using a sharp knife, cut off any uneven ends, then slice the log into 1½-inch-thick rolls and place them in the pan.

3. Let the dough rise. Cover the pan with a clean dish towel and allow the rolls to rise for about 20 to 25 minutes, or until puffy.

4. Bake. In the last few minutes of rising, preheat the oven to 350°F. Bake for 20 minutes, or until the tops start to brown lightly.

PREPARATION TIP: I love serving these with an orange cream cheese frosting, which you can make by adding 2 tablespoons of grated orange zest to plain Cream Cheese Frosting (page 175).

Cinnamon Swirl Bread

Makes 2 (9-by-5-inch) loaves

One of my favorite things in the morning is enjoying a slice
of this cinnamon bread slathered in butter. *Nut-free*

**PREP TIME: 1 hour, plus 1 hour
40 minutes to rise**
COOK TIME: 25 minutes

FOR THE DOUGH

1 cup whole milk

½ cup granulated sugar

8 tablespoons (1 stick)
  unsalted butter

1 tablespoon active
  dry yeast

4 cups all-purpose flour

1 teaspoon salt

2 large eggs, room
  temperature

2 tablespoons
  vegetable oil

FOR THE FILLING

½ cup granulated sugar

2 tablespoons ground
  cinnamon

TO MAKE THE DOUGH

1. **Combine the milk, sugar, and butter**. In a small
saucepan over medium heat, heat the milk, sugar, and
butter until the butter is melted. Remove from the heat
and cool to 110°F, then stir in the yeast. Let stand until
foamy, about 10 minutes.

2. **Add the remaining ingredients.** In a large bowl,
combine the flour and salt. Mix in the eggs, oil, and
yeast mixture. Stir until the dough pulls away from the
sides of the bowl. Place the dough on a lightly floured
surface and knead until the dough is smooth and
elastic, about 10 minutes.

3. **Allow the dough to rise.** Place the dough in a lightly
greased bowl and turn once to coat. Cover with a clean
dish towel or plastic wrap and let rise until doubled in
size, about 1 hour.

TO MAKE THE FILLING AND FINISH THE BREAD

1. **Make the filling.** In a small bowl, mix together the sugar and cinnamon.

2. **Shape the bread.** Punch down the dough. Place it on a lightly floured surface. Divide the dough in half. Roll each portion into a 16-by-8-inch rectangle. Sprinkle ¼ cup cinnamon sugar along the top, leaving ½ inch around the edges. Starting on a short side, roll up the dough. When finished, pinch along the seam to seal. Place each loaf in a greased 9-by-5-inch loaf pan, seam-side down. Allow the dough to rise again in the pan for 30 to 40 minutes, or until doubled in size and puffy.

3. **Bake.** Bake for 20 to 25 minutes, or until the bread is golden brown.

PREPARATION TIP: Sprinkle ½ cup of raisins over the cinnamon sugar before rolling up the dough to make cinnamon raisin bread.

No-Knead Cranberry-Pecan Bread

Makes 1 loaf

If you are timid about baking with yeast, this bread with sweet chewy cranberries and crunchy pecans is the perfect place to begin. *Dairy-free*

PREP TIME: **20 minutes, plus 9 hours to rise**
COOK TIME: **45 minutes**

3 cups all-purpose flour

1½ teaspoons salt

¾ teaspoon active dry yeast

¾ cup dried cranberries

¾ cup chopped pecans

1½ cups cool water

1. **Make the dough.** In a large bowl, whisk together the flour, salt, yeast, cranberries, and pecans. Make a well in the center and add the water into the well. Stir until it forms a shaggy dough.

2. **Allow the dough to rise.** Cover the bowl with a clean dish towel or plastic wrap. Allow the dough to rise until doubled in size and bubbly, 6 to 8 hours.

3. **Shape the dough.** Lightly flour a piece of parchment paper. Place the dough on the floured paper, folding the dough over on itself at least once. Shape the dough into a ball. Cover with a kitchen towel and let rise for 1 hour, or until nearly doubled in size.

4. **Preheat the oven and the Dutch oven.** About 30 minutes before the dough is finished rising, position a rack in the middle of the oven. Preheat the oven to 450°F. Place a large Dutch oven and its lid on the rack.

5. **Transfer the loaf to the Dutch oven.** Carefully set the loaf, still on the paper, in the hot Dutch oven. Make a shallow cut on the top of the dough with kitchen shears or a sharp knife so the bread can expand while baking.

6. **Bake.** Place the lid on the Dutch oven and bake, covered, for 30 minutes. Then remove the lid and bake for 15 minutes more. If you have an instant-read thermometer, insert it in the top or side to check the internal temperature. Remove the bread when it registers 210°F.

7. **Cool and slice.** Remove from the oven and use the parchment paper to lift the bread out of the Dutch oven and onto a wire rack. Let cool for at least 15 minutes before slicing.

SUBSTITUTION TIP: You can omit the cranberries and pecans altogether. Or try swapping raisins for the cranberries and walnuts for the pecans.

Basic French Bread

Makes 2 loaves

This soft bread with its crispy exterior encompasses everything
I love about homemade bread. *Dairy-free, Nut-free*

**PREP TIME: 30 minutes, plus
1 hour 40 minutes to rise**
COOK TIME: 40 minutes

5 to 6 cups all-purpose
   flour, divided

1 (¼-ounce) package
   active dry yeast

1 tablespoon granulated
   sugar

2½ teaspoons salt

2 cups water, warmed to
   105°F to 110°F

3 tablespoons
   vegetable oil

1 tablespoon cornmeal

1. **Make the dough.** In a large bowl, using a wooden spoon or a stand mixer with a dough hook attachment, combine 2 cups of flour, the yeast, sugar, and salt. Stir in the warm water and beat until well-blended. Stir in as much of the remaining flour as you can.

2. **Knead the dough.** Place the dough on a lightly floured surface and knead for 10 minutes or on low for 5 minutes in a stand mixer. Shape the dough into a ball. Place the dough in a bowl greased with the oil and turn once to coat. Cover with a clean dish towel or plastic wrap and let rise until doubled in size, about 1 hour.

3. **Shape the dough.** Punch down the dough and divide it in half. Place each half on a lightly floured surface. Cover with a clean dish towel or greased plastic wrap and let rest for 10 minutes. Roll out each half into an 8-by-12-inch rectangle. Starting on a long side, roll up each half, then tuck the ends underneath.

4. **Let the dough rise again.** Coat a large baking sheet with cooking spray and sprinkle cornmeal on the surface. Place the loaves, seam-side down, on the baking sheet. Cover with greased plastic wrap and let rise until nearly doubled in size, 35 to 40 minutes. Near the end of the rising time, preheat the oven to 375°F.

5. **Bake.** With a very sharp knife, make 3 or 4 diagonal cuts about ¼-inch deep across the top of each loaf. Bake for 35 to 40 minutes. If necessary, cover loosely with foil to prevent over-browning. Remove from the baking sheet and cool on a wire rack.

White Sandwich Bread

Makes 2 (9-by-5-inch) loaves

This soft, fluffy bread, perfect for sandwiches and toast, makes two loaves so you can enjoy one now and freeze one for later. *Dairy-free, Nut-free*

PREP TIME: 20 minutes, plus 1 hour 30 minutes to rise
COOK TIME: 30 minutes

¼ cup granulated sugar

2 cups water, warmed to 105°F to 110°F

1½ tablespoons active dry yeast

¼ cup vegetable oil

6 cups bread flour

1½ teaspoons salt

1. **Proof the yeast.** In a large bowl, using a wooden spoon or in the bowl of your stand mixer with the dough hook attachment, dissolve the sugar in the warm water. Stir in the yeast. Proof until the yeast resembles a creamy foam, about 10 minutes.

2. **Make the dough.** Add the oil, flour, and salt. Mix until the flour has been incorporated, and the dough comes away from the bowl. Place the dough on a lightly floured surface and knead for about 10 minutes or on low in a stand mixer for 5 minutes. Place the dough in a lightly greased bowl and turn once to coat. Cover the bowl with a clean dish towel or plastic wrap and let rise until doubled in size, about 1 hour.

3. **Shape the dough.** Punch down the dough and divide it in half. Roll out each half into a rectangle. Starting on the long side, roll each one up, tucking the ends underneath the loaves. Place each loaf into a greased 9-by-5-inch loaf pan. Allow the dough to rise for 30 minutes, or until the dough has risen 1 inch above pans.

4. **Preheat the oven.** Near the end of the rising time, preheat the oven to 350°F and position a rack in the middle of the oven.

5. **Bake.** Bake on the middle rack for 30 minutes, or until golden brown on top and an instant-read thermometer inserted into the bread reads 190°F. Cool completely on a wire rack before slicing.

SUBSTITUTION TIP: To make a whole-wheat sandwich bread, substitute whole-wheat flour for half of the bread flour.

Braided Challah

Makes 2 loaves

This soft braided bread will be the star of your holiday table and makes for the most wonderful French toast. *Dairy-free, Nut-free*

PREP TIME: 30 minutes, plus 2 hours 30 minutes to rise
COOK TIME: 30 minutes, plus 1 hour to cool

1 tablespoon active dry yeast

2½ cups water, warmed to 105°F to 110°F

⅓ cup granulated sugar

¼ cup vegetable oil

2 large eggs, room temperature

2 large egg yolks, room temperature

2 teaspoons salt

8 cups all-purpose flour

1 egg, beaten, for the egg wash

1 tablespoon water, for the egg wash

1. **Proof the yeast.** In a large bowl or the bowl of a stand mixer, sprinkle the yeast over the warm water. Proof until the yeast resembles a creamy foam, about 10 minutes.

2. **Make the dough.** Using a wooden spoon or the paddle attachment of a stand mixer, beat in the sugar, oil, eggs, egg yolks, and salt. Add the flour 1 cup at a time, beating after each addition.

3. **Knead the dough.** Place the dough on a lightly floured surface and knead for about 10 minutes or, using a dough hook attachment, on low for 5 minutes in a stand mixer. Place the dough into a lightly greased bowl and turn over once to coat. Cover the bowl with a clean dish towel or plastic wrap and let rise for 1½ hours, or until the dough has doubled in size.

4. **Shape the dough.** Line a baking sheet with parchment paper or coat it lightly with cooking spray. Punch down the dough and divide in half. Place each half on a lightly floured surface and knead each half for about 5 minutes, adding flour as needed to keep it from getting sticky. Divide each half into thirds and roll each third into ropes, about 1½ inches thick and 18 inches long. Firmly pinch the ends of three ropes together and braid. Place the shaped loaves on the baking sheet and loosely cover with greased plastic wrap. Allow the dough to rise for about 1 hour, or until nearly doubled in size. Toward the end of the rising time, preheat the oven to 375°F and position a rack in the middle of the oven.

5. **Make the egg wash.** Beat the egg and the water together until well combined. Brush the egg wash over each loaf.

6. **Bake.** Bake for 30 to 40 minutes, or until golden brown and an instant-read thermometer inserted into the bread reads 190°F. The bread should have a nice hollow sound when thumped on the bottom. Cool on a rack for at least 1 hour before slicing.

PREPARATION TIP: You can also sprinkle the loaves with sesame seeds or poppy seeds before baking.

Knotted Herb-Garlic Dinner Rolls

Makes 24 rolls

During my freshman year of college, I lived off zesty garlic herb breadsticks.
These knotted dinner rolls are my grown-up version, and equally delicious.

**PREP TIME: 25 minutes, plus
45 minutes to rise**
COOK TIME: 25 minutes

FOR THE DOUGH

½ cup water, warmed to
    105°F to 110°F

2 cups milk

3 tablespoons unsalted
    butter, melted

1 tablespoon granulated
    sugar

2 teaspoons salt

1 teaspoon garlic powder

¼ cup shredded
    Parmesan cheese

2½ tablespoons instant
    yeast

6 to 7 cups all-purpose
    flour, divided

TO MAKE THE DOUGH

1. Proof the yeast. Combine the water, milk, butter, sugar, salt, garlic powder, Parmesan cheese, and yeast in a large bowl or the bowl of a stand mixer. Using a wooden spoon or the paddle attachment of a stand mixer, stir well. Let sit for 6 to 8 minutes, or until the yeast begins to foam.

2. Make the dough. Add 5 cups of the flour and mix until the dough forms a rough, shaggy mass.

3. Knead the dough. Using a wooden spoon or a dough hook attachment of a stand mixer, stir in the remaining flour, ½ cup at a time, until a smooth ball begins to form. Place on a lightly floured work surface and knead by hand for about 10 minutes or on low for about 5 minutes in a stand mixer. The dough should feel elastic and slightly sticky to the touch.

4. Allow the dough to rise. Place the dough into a lightly greased bowl and turn over once to coat. Cover with a clean dish cloth or plastic wrap and let rise for 20 minutes, or until the dough is full and puffy.

5. Shape the rolls. Punch down the dough and pat it out into an 8-by-12-inch rectangle. Cut the dough into 4 long strips, then cut each strip into 6 portions for a total of 24 portions. Roll each portion into a 10-inch rope and twist the rope into a simple knot.

6. Allow a second rise. Line two baking sheets with parchment paper or silicone baking mats. Place the rolls on the baking sheets. Cover with greased plastic wrap and let rise for 20 to 25 minutes, or until puffy.

FOR THE TOPPING

4 tablespoons (½ stick) salted butter, melted

¼ cup shredded Parmesan cheese

1 teaspoon garlic powder

1 tablespoon minced fresh parsley or 1 teaspoon dried parsley

7. Preheat the oven. During the last few minutes of rising time, preheat the oven to 350°F.

8. Bake the rolls. Bake the rolls for 20 to 25 minutes, until golden brown and an instant-read thermometer inserted into a roll reads 190°F.

TO MAKE THE TOPPING

Make the topping. While rolls are baking, prepare the topping. In a small bowl, mix together all the topping ingredients. Brush the topping over the rolls immediately when they are finished baking.

SUBSTITUTION TIP: To make plain dinner rolls, omit the Parmesan cheese and garlic powder in the dough and instead of using the topping, simply brush the rolls with melted butter when they come out of the oven.

Berry Buttercream PAGE 178

Fantastic Frostings and Glazes

Powdered Sugar Glaze 170

Chocolate Ganache 171

Fudge Icing 172

Caramel Icing 173

Fluffy White (Boiled Milk) Icing 174

Cream Cheese Frosting 175

Vanilla Buttercream 176

Coconut Buttercream 177

Berry Buttercream 178

Stabilized Whipped Cream 179

Seven-Minute Icing 180

Swiss Meringue Buttercream 181

Italian Meringue Buttercream 182

Powdered Sugar Glaze

Makes 1 cup

Whenever I need an easy, sweet glaze for a delicious treat, I turn
to this vanilla glaze made with powdered sugar. *Nut-free*

PREP TIME: **5 minutes**

2 cups powdered sugar

3 tablespoons milk

1½ teaspoons vanilla
extract

Mix all the ingredients. In a medium bowl, whisk
together all the ingredients until smooth and
well combined.

SUBSTITUTION TIP: Add 3 tablespoons of cocoa
powder to turn this into a chocolate glaze.

Chocolate Ganache

Makes 1 cup

Although it may look and sound fancy, ganache is easy to make—nothing more than two simple ingredients combined to make a glossy, rich glaze. *Gluten-free, Nut-free*

PREP TIME: **5 minutes**
COOK TIME: **1 minute in the microwave or 2 to 3 minutes on the stove**

1 cup heavy cream

1⅓ cups (8 ounces) bittersweet or semisweet chocolate (chips or chopped)

1. **Heat the cream.** In a small saucepan, heat the cream over low heat until simmering, 2 to 3 minutes. If using a microwave, heat for 30 seconds to 1 minute in a microwave-safe bowl. The cream can bubble over, so watch it closely.

2. **Combine the cream and chocolate.** When the cream is heated, pour it over the chocolate and let the mixture sit for 3 to 5 minutes. Whisk until smooth. Allow the ganache to cool slightly before using. If you want a thicker ganache, allow it to cool longer.

PREPARATION TIP: If you want to turn this into a frosting, allow it to cool completely, then, using an electric mixer, beat it until light and fluffy.

Fudge Icing

Makes 2 cups

This magical chocolate frosting, composed of six simple ingredients, is made on the stovetop. The result is a glossy, fudgy icing that can be poured over a cake and that sets in seconds. *Gluten-free, Nut-free*

PREP TIME: **5 minutes**
COOK TIME: **5 minutes**

1 cup granulated sugar

¼ cup unsweetened cocoa powder

⅓ cup milk

5 tablespoons unsalted butter

¼ teaspoon salt

1 teaspoon vanilla extract

1. **Combine the ingredients.** In a small saucepan over low heat, combine the sugar, cocoa powder, milk, butter, and salt. Heat until the sugar is dissolved.

2. **Boil the mixture.** Bring the mixture to a rolling boil, whisking constantly for 2 minutes.

3. **Add the vanilla.** Remove from the heat. Add the vanilla and continue whisking until it starts to thicken slightly. The icing will be very creamy. Pour over your cake immediately—it will set quickly.

SUBSTITUTION TIP: Try adding ½ teaspoon of peppermint extract for a mint chocolate icing.

Caramel Icing

Makes 2 cups

This icing is made on the stovetop with brown sugar and a touch of vanilla extract. It comes together very quickly. *Nut-free*

PREP TIME: 5 minutes
COOK TIME: 5 minutes

4 tablespoons (½ stick) unsalted butter, room temperature

½ cup light brown sugar

⅓ cup heavy cream

½ teaspoon vanilla extract

½ teaspoon salt

1 cup powdered sugar

1. **Combine the first three ingredients.** In a small saucepan over medium heat, combine the butter, brown sugar, and cream. Bring to a boil, whisking constantly.

2. **Add the vanilla.** Remove from the heat and add the vanilla and salt. Let cool for 5 minutes.

3. **Add the powdered sugar.** Stir in the powdered sugar and pour over your cake immediately.

SUBSTITUTION TIP: You can substitute milk for the heavy cream. The icing won't be as rich, but it will still be creamy and delicious.

Fluffy White (Boiled Milk) Icing

Makes 3 cups

This fluffy buttercream goes by many names—boiled milk
icing, flour buttercream, and ermine icing. It is the traditional
buttercream to serve on red velvet cake. *Nut-free*

PREP TIME: **25 minutes**

4½ tablespoons
    all-purpose flour

1 cup whole milk

1 cup granulated sugar

1 teaspoon vanilla extract

⅛ teaspoon salt

1 cup (2 sticks)
    unsalted butter,
    room temperature

1. Combine the first three ingredients. In a small
saucepan set over medium heat, whisk together the
flour, milk, and sugar and heat to a simmer. Stir frequently until it becomes very thick, like a pudding.

2. Add the vanilla. Remove from the heat and whisk
in the vanilla and salt. Pour the mixture into a medium
bowl to allow it to cool completely. Put plastic wrap
on the surface to keep a skin from forming. (This
portion of the recipe can be made up to a day ahead
of time and refrigerated. Bring to room temperature
before proceeding.)

3. Whip the butter. In a large bowl, using an electric
mixer set on medium, whip the butter until light and
fluffy, scraping the sides of the bowl occasionally, about
5 minutes.

4. Add the flour mixture. With the mixer on medium,
add the room-temperature flour mixture 1 tablespoon
at a time. Continue to beat until the icing becomes light
and fluffy.

TROUBLESHOOTING TIP: Make sure your flour mixture
is at room temperature before using it, so as not to melt
or curdle the butter.

Cream Cheese Frosting

Makes 3 to 4 cups

This sweet and tangy cream cheese frosting is easy to make and perfect for using on a carrot cake or red velvet cupcakes. *Nut-free*

PREP TIME: 5 minutes

1 cup cream cheese, room temperature

8 tablespoons (1 stick) unsalted butter, room temperature

3 cups powdered sugar

⅛ teaspoon salt

2 teaspoons vanilla extract

1. **Mix the cream cheese and butter.** In a large bowl, using an electric mixer set on low, combine the cream cheese and butter. Increase the speed to medium and beat until smooth, 1 to 2 minutes.

2. **Add the powdered sugar.** Reduce the mixer speed to low and add the powdered sugar, 1 cup at a time. Mix until all of the sugar is fully incorporated.

3. **Add the salt and vanilla.** Add the salt and vanilla and mix to combine.

INGREDIENT TIP: Be sure to use a block of full-fat cream cheese, not low-fat cream cheese or cream cheese spread, because these would give the frosting a runny consistency.

Vanilla Buttercream

Makes 3 to 4 cups

I grew up on canned buttercream frosting, so I wasn't a fan until I made this heavenly creamy frosting with just a few simple ingredients. *Nut-free*

PREP TIME: 10 minutes

1½ cups (3 sticks) unsalted butter, room temperature

3 cups powdered sugar

2 to 3 tablespoons heavy cream or milk

2½ teaspoons vanilla extract

⅛ teaspoon salt

1. **Mix butter and sugar.** In a large bowl, using an electric mixer set on low, combine the butter and powdered sugar. Once the sugar begins to be incorporated, increase speed to medium and mix until combined.

2. **Add the remaining ingredients.** Add the cream, vanilla, and salt and mix on medium to high speed for 7 to 8 minutes, until light and creamy.

SUBSTITUTION TIP: Make Chocolate Buttercream by mixing in ½ cup of cocoa powder at the end.

Coconut Buttercream

Makes 3 to 4 cups

Every coconut cake needs a silky coconut buttercream frosting, like this recipe made with coconut extract and shredded coconut. *Nut-free*

PREP TIME: 10 minutes

1¼ cups (2½ sticks) unsalted butter, room temperature

2½ cups powdered sugar

2 tablespoons heavy cream

1 teaspoon vanilla extract

2 teaspoons coconut extract

⅛ teaspoon salt

1 cup shredded sweetened coconut

1. **Combine the butter and powdered sugar.** In a large bowl, using an electric mixer set on low, combine the butter and powdered sugar. After the powdered sugar begins to get incorporated, increase speed to medium until combined.

2. **Add the cream, extracts, and salt.** Add the cream, vanilla, coconut extract, and salt. Mix on medium to high speed for 8 minutes, or until light and creamy.

3. **Stir in the coconut.** Using a rubber spatula, stir in the coconut.

SUBSTITUTION TIP: Instead of coconut extract, you can use 5 to 6 tablespoons of canned coconut milk or 2 to 3 tablespoons of coconut cream.

Berry Buttercream

Makes 3 to 4 cups

The key to this buttercream is cooking the berries first so all the flavor from the purée can create a summery, sweet flavor for your buttercream. *Nut-free*

PREP TIME: 10 minutes
COOK TIME: 10 minutes

1½ cups berries, fresh or frozen

1½ cups (3 sticks) unsalted butter, room temperature

3 cups powdered sugar

2 to 3 tablespoons heavy cream or milk

2½ teaspoons vanilla extract

⅛ teaspoon salt

1. **Make the berry purée.** In a saucepan over medium heat, cook the berries. Mash the berries until smooth. Simmer until reduced to about ½ cup of liquid.

2. **Strain the purée.** Remove from the heat. Strain the purée through a sieve set over a bowl. Cool before adding to buttercream.

3. **Mix the butter and sugar.** In a large bowl, using an electric mixer set on low, mix the butter and powdered sugar. When the sugar begins to get incorporated, increase the speed to medium and mix until well combined.

4. **Add the cream, vanilla, and salt.** Add the cream, vanilla, and salt and mix on medium-high for 8 minutes, or until light and creamy.

5. **Add the purée.** Mix in ¼ cup of purée or more to taste.

SUBSTITUTION TIP: Make this berry buttercream with any type of berry—just keep the total amount to 1½ cups.

Stabilized Whipped Cream

Makes 2 cups

I love making this version of whipped cream because it lasts for hours thanks to a secret ingredient. *Gluten-free, Nut-free*

PREP TIME: 10 minutes

4 teaspoons cold water

1 teaspoon unflavored gelatin

1 cup cold heavy cream

½ cup powdered sugar

½ teaspoon vanilla extract

1. **Combine the water and gelatin.** Pour the water into a small microwave-safe bowl and sprinkle the gelatin over it. Let it sit for 5 minutes.

2. **Combine the remaining ingredients.** While the gelatin is sitting, put the cream, powdered sugar, and vanilla into a medium bowl.

3. **Heat the gelatin.** When the gelatin is set, place it in the microwave and heat until it turns to liquid, about 10 seconds.

4. **Beat the cream.** Using an electric mixer set on low, start beating the cream. Increase the speed to high. Slowly pour the melted gelatin into the cream in a small steady stream. Continue beating the cream until medium-stiff peaks form.

SUBSTITUTION TIP: Add 1 to 2 tablespoons of cocoa powder in step 4 to make a chocolate whipped cream.

Seven-Minute Icing

Makes 2 cups

This icing, so named because it takes seven minutes to mix egg whites into a fluffy meringue, is like eating a soft cloud of marshmallow. *Dairy-free, Gluten-free, Nut-free*

PREP TIME: **15 minutes**
COOK TIME: **7 minutes**

1½ cups granulated sugar

⅓ cup cold water

2 large egg whites, room temperature

¼ teaspoon cream of tartar

¼ teaspoon salt

1½ teaspoons vanilla extract

1. **Combine the ingredients.** Set a small saucepan or the bottom of a double boiler filled with about two inches of water over medium heat and bring to a simmer. In a heat-proof bowl or the top of a double boiler, combine the sugar, water, egg whites, cream of tartar, and salt.

2. **Mix the icing.** Using an electric mixer set on low, beat the egg white mixture for 30 seconds. Set the bowl over the saucepan of simmering water. Be sure the bottom of the bowl does not touch the simmering water. Continue beating at high speed for about 7 minutes, or until the egg whites are stiff and glossy.

3. **Add the vanilla.** Remove from the heat, add the vanilla, and beat for another 1 to 2 minutes. Use this frosting right away, as it will set quickly.

SUBSTITUTION TIP: You can use 2 teaspoons of corn syrup instead of the cream of tartar. Try an extract other than vanilla to give this a different flavor.

Swiss Meringue Buttercream

Makes 5 cups

If you think traditional buttercream made with powdered sugar is too sweet, this might the buttercream for you. *Gluten-free, Nut-free*

PREP TIME: 20 minutes
COOK TIME: 5 minutes

5 egg whites, room temperature

¾ cup granulated sugar

1½ cups (3 sticks) unsalted butter, room temperature and cut into tablespoons

2 teaspoons vanilla extract

¼ teaspoon salt

1. **Combine the egg whites and sugar.** Put the egg whites and sugar in a large, clean, dry mixing bowl set over simmering water. Whisk constantly until the sugar melts and the mixture is very thin and warm, about 5 minutes. Feel the mixture between your fingertips. If the mixture still feels grainy, continue to warm it. Be sure the bottom of the bowl does not come in contact with the water.

2. **Whip the egg whites.** Remove the bowl from the heat and, using an electric mixer fitted with a whisk attachment and set on high, whip the egg whites and sugar until stiff peaks form, about 5 minutes. Reduce the speed to low and continue beating until cool. Feel the bottom of the bowl to make sure it is cool to the touch before adding the butter.

3. **Add the butter.** Beat in small pieces of softened butter on medium speed. The mixture may curdle before coming together. Add the vanilla and salt and mix.

TROUBLESHOOTING TIP: If the buttercream has completely separated, place the bowl in the refrigerator for 10 to 15 minutes, then try whipping again.

Italian Meringue Buttercream

Makes 5 cups

Italian meringue buttercream is the silkiest buttercream
ever and holds up well in warmer conditions, so it's a
perfect frosting for outdoor events. *Nut-free*

PREP TIME: **20 minutes**
COOK TIME: **5 minutes**

3 cups powdered sugar

⅔ cup water

5 large egg whites, room
temperature

⅛ teaspoon cream of
tartar

1½ cups (3 sticks)
unsalted butter,
room temperature and
cut into tablespoons

2 teaspoons vanilla
extract

1. **Boil the sugar and water.** In a small saucepan over medium heat, bring the powdered sugar and water to a boil. Do not stir. Continue boiling until the syrup reaches 238°F on a candy thermometer.

2. **Whip the egg whites.** In a large, clean, dry bowl, using an electric mixer fitted with a whisk attachment and set on low, whip the egg whites until foamy. Add the cream of tartar, and beat on medium-high speed until stiff but not dry; do not overbeat.

3. **Add the sugar syrup.** With the mixer on high, add the hot syrup to the egg whites in a steady stream. Continue beating until the mixture is no longer steaming, about 3 minutes. Feel the bottom of the mixing bowl to ensure the mixture is not warm before adding the butter. If the mixture is too warm, the butter will melt.

4. **Add the butter.** Add the butter 1 tablespoon at a time, beating until spreadable, 3 to 5 minutes. Then beat in the vanilla. If the icing curdles, keep beating until smooth.

TROUBLESHOOTING TIP: You want a clean grease-free bowl to whip your egg whites. Any grease will inhibit the egg whites from whipping up properly.

Measurement Conversions

VOLUME EQUIVALENTS (LIQUID)

US STANDARD	US STANDARD (OUNCES)	METRIC (APPROXIMATE)
2 tablespoons	1 fl. oz.	30 mL
¼ cup	2 fl. oz.	60 mL
½ cup	4 fl. oz.	120 mL
1 cup	8 fl. oz.	240 mL
1½ cups	12 fl. oz.	355 mL
2 cups or 1 pint	16 fl. oz.	475 mL
4 cups or 1 quart	32 fl. oz.	1 L
1 gallon	128 fl. oz.	4 L

OVEN TEMPERATURES

FAHRENHEIT (F)	CELSIUS (C) (APPROXIMATE)
250°F	120°C
300°F	150°C
325°F	165°C
350°F	180°C
375°F	190°C
400°F	200°C
425°F	220°C
450°F	230°C

VOLUME EQUIVALENTS (DRY)

US STANDARD	METRIC (APPROXIMATE)
⅛ teaspoon	0.5 mL
¼ teaspoon	1 mL
½ teaspoon	2 mL
¾ teaspoon	4 mL
1 teaspoon	5 mL
1 tablespoon	15 mL
¼ cup	59 mL
⅓ cup	79 mL
½ cup	118 mL
⅔ cup	156 mL
¾ cup	177 mL
1 cup	235 mL
2 cups or 1 pint	475 mL
3 cups	700 mL
4 cups or 1 quart	1 L

WEIGHT EQUIVALENTS

US STANDARD	METRIC (APPROXIMATE)
½ ounce	15 g
1 ounce	30 g
2 ounces	60 g
4 ounces	115 g
8 ounces	225 g
12 ounces	340 g
16 ounces or 1 pound	455 g

The Dirty Dozen and The Clean Fifteen™

A nonprofit environmental watchdog organization called Environmental Working Group (EWG) looks at data supplied by the US Department of Agriculture (USDA) and the Food and Drug Administration (FDA) about pesticide residues. Each year it compiles a list of the best and worst pesticide loads found in commercial crops. You can use these lists to decide which fruits and vegetables to buy organic to minimize your exposure to pesticides and which produce is considered safe enough to buy conventionally. This does not mean they are pesticide-free, though, so wash these fruits and vegetables thoroughly. The list is updated annually, and you can find it online at EWG.org/FoodNews.

Dirty Dozen™

- strawberries
- spinach
- kale
- nectarines
- apples
- grapes
- peaches
- cherries
- pears
- tomatoes
- celery
- potatoes

†Additionally, nearly three-quarters of hot pepper samples contained pesticide residues.

Clean Fifteen™

- avocados
- sweet corn*
- pineapples
- sweet peas (frozen)
- onions
- papayas*
- eggplants
- asparagus
- kiwis
- cabbages
- cauliflower
- cantaloupes
- broccoli
- mushrooms
- honeydew melons

* A small amount of sweet corn, papaya, and summer squash sold in the United States is produced from genetically modified seeds. Buy organic varieties of these crops if you want to avoid genetically modified produce.

Resources

Books, Magazines, and Websites

America's Test Kitchen. *Cook's Illustrated Baking Book*. Boston: America's Test Kitchen, 2018.

Bake from Scratch Magazine: BakeFromScratch.com

Handle the Heat: HandleTheHeat.com

King Arthur Flour. *King Arthur Flour Baker's Companion: The All-Purpose Baking Cookbook*. New York: The Countryman Press, 2003.

Sally's Baking Addiction: SallysBakingAddiction.com

Ingredients, Tools, and Stores

McCormick Spices: McCormick.com

Oxo: Oxo.com

Red Star Yeast: RedStarYeast.com

Sur La Table: SurLaTable.com

Index

A

Apples
Apple-Cinnamon
Scones, 153
Apple Pie Bars, 55
Apple Streusel Pie, 64
Apple-Walnut Cake, 130
Blueberry Crumble
Pie, 66–67
Appliances, 5

B

Bacon
Bacon and Swiss Quiche, 91
Maple-Bacon Cupcakes, 119
Maple-Bacon Scones, 154
Bakeware, 4
Baking pans, 4
Baking powder, 6
Baking sheets, 4
Baking soda, 6
Bananas
Banana Bread, 101
Banana Cream Pie, 76–77
Banana Cupcakes, 117
Banoffee Bars, 50
Hummingbird Layer
Cake, 136
Banoffee Bars, 50

Bars. *See also* Brownies
Apple Pie Bars, 55
Banoffee Bars, 50
Butterscotch Blondies, 46
Cookies and Cream
Bars, 45
Frosted Sugar Cookie
Bars, 44
Lemon Bars, 53
Maple-Peach Bars, 49
Oatmeal Chocolate Chip
Cookie Bars, 51
Pecan Pie Bars, 54
Pumpkin Bars, 48
Raspberry Jam Bars, 56
S'mores Bars, 52
Basic French Bread, 162
Basic Pie Dough with Sweet
Pie Dough Option, 60
Beer Bread, Cheesy, 106
Berries
Berry Buttercream, 178
Berry White Chocolate
Tart, 88
Blueberry Crumble
Pie, 66–67
Blueberry-Lemon Coffee
Cake, 129
Blueberry Muffins, 96

Cranberry-Orange
Bread, 105
Cranberry-Pear Crumble
Pie, 65
Lemon-Raspberry Layer
Cake, 137
Mixed Berry Galette, 83–84
No-Knead
Cranberry-Pecan Bread,
160–161
Peach-Blueberry Tart, 86
Raspberry-Almond
Thumbprints, 24
Raspberry Cheesecake
Brownies, 57
Raspberry Jam Bars, 56
Strawberry Bread, 103
Strawberry-Rhubarb
Galette, 82
Biscuits
Buttermilk Biscuits, 149
Jalapeño-Cheddar
Biscuits, 151
Shortcake Biscuits, 152
Whole-Wheat Biscuits, 150
Black Bottom Peanut Butter
Mousse Pie, 74–75
Blueberry Crumble
Pie, 66–67

Blueberry-Lemon Coffee
    Cake, 129
Blueberry Muffins, 96
Braided Challah, 164–165
Breads. *See also* Quick breads
    Basic French Bread, 162
    Braided Challah, 164–165
    Cinnamon Swirl Bread,
        158–159
    No-Knead
        Cranberry-Pecan Bread,
        160–161
    White Sandwich Bread, 163
Brownie Pie, 62
Brownies
    Fudgy Chocolate
        Brownies, 47
    Raspberry Cheesecake
        Brownies, 57
Bundt cake pan, 4
Butter, 6
    creaming with sugar, 13
    cutting into flour, 16
Buttercream
    Berry Buttercream, 178
    Coconut Buttercream, 177
    Fluffy White (Boiled Milk)
        Icing, 174
    Italian Meringue
        Buttercream, 182
    Swiss Meringue
        Buttercream, 181
    Vanilla Buttercream, 176
Buttermilk Biscuits, 149
Butterscotch Blondies, 46
Buttery Round Crackers,
    140–141

C

Cakes. *See also* Cupcakes
    Apple-Walnut Cake, 130
    Blueberry-Lemon Coffee
        Cake, 129
    Carrot Sheet Cake, 123
    Chocolate Layer Cake, 133
    Chocolate Pudding
        Cake, 126
    Chocolate Zucchini
        Cake, 127
    Cinnamon Roll Cake, 122
    Coconut Layer Cake, 135
    Gingerbread Cake, 121
    Hummingbird Layer
        Cake, 136
    Lemon-Raspberry Layer
        Cake, 137
    Orange Pound Cake, 125
    Pineapple Upside-Down
        Cake, 131
    Pumpkin Cake, 124
    Red Velvet Layer Cake, 134
    Summer Peach Crumb
        Cake, 128
    Vanilla Layer Cake, 132
Caprese Galette, 85
Caramel Icing, 173
Caramel sauce
    Banoffee Bars, 50
Carrot Cake and
        Oatmeal Cookie
        Sandwiches, 40–41
Carrot Sheet Cake, 123
Cheese
    Bacon and Swiss Quiche, 91
    Caprese Galette, 85

Cheesy Beer Bread, 106
Garlic-Parmesan
    Crackers, 148
Homemade Cheddar
    Cheese Crackers, 143
Jalapeño-Cheddar
    Biscuits, 151
Knotted Herb-Garlic
    Dinner Rolls, 166–167
Mushroom Quiche, 92
Sausage and Spinach
    Quiche, 93
Savory Cheddar and Herb
    Muffins, 99
Summer Vegetable
    Tart, 89–90
Cherries
    Fresh Cherry Pie, 70–71
    Pineapple Upside-Down
        Cake, 131
Chocolate, 7. *See also* White
    chocolate
    Black Bottom Peanut
        Butter Mousse Pie, 74–75
    Brownie Pie, 62
    Chocolate Brownie
        Cookies, 34
    Chocolate Cream
        Pie, 72–73
    Chocolate Cupcakes, 115
    Chocolate Ganache, 171
    Chocolate Layer Cake, 133
    Chocolate Pecan Pie, 63
    Chocolate Pudding
        Cake, 126
    Chocolate Zucchini
        Cake, 127

Cookies and Cream Bars, 45

Double Chocolate Chip
    Bread, 109

Espresso and Chocolate
    Chip Shortbread, 25

Fudge Icing, 172

Fudgy Chocolate
    Brownies, 47

melting, 16

Monster Cookies, 36

Oatmeal Chocolate Chip
    Cookie Bars, 51

Oatmeal Cookies, 30

Perfect Chocolate Chip
    Cookies, 31

Raspberry Cheesecake
    Brownies, 57

Red Velvet Chocolate Chip
    Cookies, 37

Red Velvet Layer Cake, 134

S'mores Bars, 52

Spiced Hot Chocolate
    Cookies, 35

Cinnamon Roll Cake, 122

Cinnamon Swirl Bread,
    158–159

Cinnamon Swirl Bread (quick
    bread), 110

Coconut

    Carrot Cake and
        Oatmeal Cookie
        Sandwiches, 40–41

    Coconut Bread, 102

    Coconut Buttercream, 177

    Coconut Cream Pie, 78–79

    Coconut Layer Cake, 135

    Coconut Macaroons, 27

Coffee Cake Muffins, 98

Cookies, 25. *See also* Bars

    Carrot Cake and
        Oatmeal Cookie
        Sandwiches, 40–41

    Chocolate Brownie
        Cookies, 34

    Coconut Macaroons, 27

    Easy Sugar Cookies, 22

    Glazed Orange Ricotta
        Cookies, 39

    Iced Lime Meltaways, 38

    Maple Cookies, 26

    Monster Cookies, 36

    Oatmeal Cookies, 30

    Perfect Chocolate Chip
        Cookies, 31

    Pistachio Cookies, 32

    Pumpkin and White
        Chocolate Chip
        Cookies, 33

    Raspberry-Almond
        Thumbprints, 24

    Red Velvet Chocolate Chip
        Cookies, 37

    Snickerdoodles, 23

    Soft Molasses Cookies, 28

    Soft Peanut Butter
        Cookies, 29

    Spiced Hot Chocolate
        Cookies, 35

Cookies and Cream Bars, 45

Cookie scoop, 5

Cookware, 4

Cooling, 9

Cooling rack, 4

Cornbread, Honey, 107

Crackers

    Buttery Round Crackers,
        140–141

    Garlic-Parmesan
        Crackers, 148

    Graham Crackers, 146

    Homemade Cheddar
        Cheese Crackers, 143

    Olive Oil Flatbread
        Crackers, 144

    Saltine Crackers, 145

    Spicy Chili Crackers, 147

    Whole-Wheat
        Crackers, 142

Cranberry-Orange
    Bread, 105

Cranberry-Pear Crumble
    Pie, 65

Cream cheese

    Berry White Chocolate
        Tart, 88

    Black Bottom Peanut
        Butter Mousse Pie,
        74–75

    Carrot Cake and
        Oatmeal Cookie
        Sandwiches, 40–41

    Cookies and Cream
        Bars, 45

    Cream Cheese
        Frosting, 175

    Lemon Cheesecake
        Tart, 87

    Raspberry Cheesecake
        Brownies, 57

Creaming butter and
    sugar, 13

Cupcakes
  Banana Cupcakes, 117
  Chocolate Cupcakes, 115
  Lemon Cupcakes, 116
  Maple-Bacon Cupcakes, 119
  Peanut Butter
    Cupcakes, 118
  Snickerdoodle
    Cupcakes, 120
  Vanilla Cupcakes, 114
Cutting in, 16

D

Dairy-free
  Basic French Bread, 162
  Braided Challah, 164–165
  Coconut Macaroons, 27
  No-Knead Cranberry-Pecan
    Bread, 160–161
  Olive Oil Flatbread
    Crackers, 144
  Seven-Minute Icing, 180
  Spicy Chili Crackers, 147
  White Sandwich Bread, 163
Doneness, 8–9
Double Chocolate Chip
    Bread, 109
Dough
  Basic Pie Dough with Sweet
    Pie Dough Option, 60
  kneading, 14

E

Easy Sugar Cookies, 22
Eggs
  Bacon and Swiss Quiche, 91
  Banana Cream Pie, 76–77

Braided Challah, 164–165
Chocolate Cream Pie, 72–73
Coconut Cream Pie, 78–79
Coconut Macaroons, 27
Italian Meringue
    Buttercream, 182
Lemon Bars, 53
Lemon Cheesecake Tart, 87
Lemon Meringue
    Pie, 80–81
Mushroom Quiche, 92
Pecan Pie Bars, 54
Sausage and Spinach
    Quiche, 93
separating, 8
Seven-Minute Icing, 180
Swiss Meringue
    Buttercream, 181
whipping egg whites, 15
Equipment, 4–5
Espresso and Chocolate Chip
    Shortbread, 25

F

Fats, 6
Flours, 5
  cutting butter into, 16
  measuring, 8
Fluffy White (Boiled Milk)
    Icing, 174
Folding, 12
Food processors, 5
Fresh Cherry Pie, 70–71
Frosted Sugar Cookie Bars, 44
Frostings. *See also* Glazes
  Berry Buttercream, 178
  Caramel Icing, 173

Coconut Buttercream, 177
Cream Cheese Frosting, 175
Fluffy White (Boiled Milk)
    Icing, 174
Fudge Icing, 172
Italian Meringue
    Buttercream, 182
Seven-Minute Icing, 180
Swiss Meringue
    Buttercream, 181
Vanilla Buttercream, 176
Fudge Icing, 172
Fudgy Chocolate Brownies, 47

G

Galettes
  Caprese Galette, 85
  Mixed Berry Galette, 83–84
  Strawberry-Rhubarb
    Galette, 82
Garlic-Parmesan
    Crackers, 148
Gingerbread Cake, 121
Glazed Orange Ricotta
    Cookies, 39
Glazes
  Chocolate Ganache, 171
  Powdered Sugar Glaze, 170
Gluten-free
  Chocolate Ganache, 171
  Coconut Macaroons, 27
  Fudge Icing, 172
  Seven-Minute Icing, 180
  Stabilized Whipped
    Cream, 179
  Swiss Meringue
    Buttercream, 181

Graham crackers
    Banana Cream Pie, 76–77
    Graham Crackers
        (recipe), 146
    Key Lime Pie, 61
    Lemon Cheesecake Tart, 87
    S'mores Bars, 52

H

Herbs, fresh
    Caprese Galette, 85
    Knotted Herb-Garlic
        Dinner Rolls, 166–167
    Savory Cheddar and Herb
        Muffins, 99
    Summer Vegetable
        Tart, 89–90
Homemade Cheddar Cheese
    Crackers, 143
Honey Cornbread, 107
Hummingbird Layer
    Cake, 136

I

Iced Lime Meltaways, 38
Ingredients, 5–7
Irish Soda Bread, 108
Italian Meringue
    Buttercream, 182

J

Jalapeño-Cheddar
    Biscuits, 151

K

Key Lime Pie, 61
Kneading, 14

Knotted Herb-Garlic Dinner
    Rolls, 166–167

L

Leavening agents, 6
Lemons
    Blueberry-Lemon Coffee
        Cake, 129
    Lemon Bars, 53
    Lemon Cheesecake
        Tart, 87
    Lemon Cupcakes, 116
    Lemon Meringue
        Pie, 80–81
    Lemon and Poppy Seed
        Bread, 104
    Lemon-Raspberry Layer
        Cake, 137
Limes
    Iced Lime Meltaways, 38
    Key Lime Pie, 61

M

Maple-Bacon Cupcakes, 119
Maple-Bacon Scones, 154
Maple Cookies, 26
Maple-Peach Bars, 49
Marshmallows
    S'mores Bars, 52
Measuring ingredients, 8
Measuring tools, 4
Microplane rasp graters, 5
Mise en place, 7
Mixed Berry Galette, 83–84
Mixers, 5
Mixing, 8, 12
Mixing tools, 4

Molasses
    Gingerbread Cake, 121
    Soft Molasses Cookies, 28
Monster Cookies, 36
Muffins
    Blueberry Muffins, 96
    Coffee Cake Muffins, 98
    Orange Muffins, 97
    Savory Cheddar and Herb
        Muffins, 99
Mushroom Quiche, 92

N

No-Knead Cranberry-Pecan
    Bread, 160–161
Nut-free
    Apple-Cinnamon
        Scones, 153
    Apple Pie Bars, 55
    Apple Streusel Pie, 64
    Bacon and Swiss Quiche, 91
    Banana Cream Pie, 76–77
    Banana Cupcakes, 117
    Banoffee Bars, 50
    Basic French Bread, 162
    Basic Pie Dough with Sweet
        Pie Dough Option, 60
    Berry White Chocolate
        Tart, 88
    Blueberry Crumble
        Pie, 66–67
    Blueberry-Lemon Coffee
        Cake, 129
    Blueberry Muffins, 96
    Braided Challah, 164–165
    Brownie Pie, 62
    Buttermilk Biscuits, 149

Nut-free *(Continued)*

Butterscotch Blondies, 46

Caprese Galette, 85

Caramel Icing, 173

Carrot Sheet Cake, 123

Cheesy Beer Bread, 106

Chocolate Brownie
 Cookies, 34

Chocolate Cream
 Pie, 72–73

Chocolate Cupcakes, 115

Chocolate Ganache, 171

Chocolate Layer Cake, 133

Chocolate Pudding
 Cake, 126

Chocolate Zucchini
 Cake, 127

Cinnamon Roll Cake, 122

Cinnamon Swirl Bread,
 158–159

Cinnamon Swirl Bread
 (quick bread), 110

Coconut Bread, 102

Coconut Buttercream, 177

Coconut Cream Pie, 78–79

Coconut Layer Cake, 135

Coffee Cake Muffins, 98

Cookies and Cream
 Bars, 45

Cranberry-Orange
 Bread, 105

Cranberry-Pear Crumble
 Pie, 65

Cream Cheese Frosting, 175

Double Chocolate Chip
 Bread, 109

Easy Sugar Cookies, 23

Espresso and Chocolate
 Chip Shortbread, 25

Fluffy White (Boiled Milk)
 Icing, 174

Frosted Sugar Cookie
 Bars, 44

Fudge Icing, 172

Garlic-Parmesan
 Crackers, 148

Gingerbread Cake, 121

Glazed Orange Ricotta
 Cookies, 39

Graham Crackers, 146

Homemade Cheddar
 Cheese Crackers, 143

Honey Cornbread, 107

Iced Lime Meltaways, 38

Irish Soda Bread, 108

Italian Meringue
 Buttercream, 182

Jalapeño-Cheddar
 Biscuits, 151

Key Lime Pie, 61

Lemon Bars, 53

Lemon Cheesecake
 Tart, 87

Lemon Cupcakes, 116

Lemon Meringue
 Pie, 80–81

Lemon and Poppy Seed
 Bread, 104

Lemon-Raspberry Layer
 Cake, 137

Maple-Bacon
 Cupcakes, 119

Maple-Bacon Scones, 154

Maple Cookies, 26

Maple-Peach Bars, 49

Mixed Berry Galette, 83–84

Mushroom Quiche, 92

Oatmeal Chocolate Chip
 Cookie Bars, 51

Oatmeal Cookies, 30

Olive Oil Flatbread
 Crackers, 144

Orange Muffins, 97

Orange Sweet Rolls,
 156–157

Peach-Blueberry Tart, 86

Perfect Chocolate Chip
 Cookies, 31

Pineapple Upside-Down
 Cake, 131

Powdered Sugar Glaze, 170

Pumpkin and White
 Chocolate Chip
 Cookies, 33

Pumpkin Cake, 124

Raspberry Cheesecake
 Brownies, 57

Raspberry Jam Bars, 56

Red Velvet Layer Cake, 134

Saltine Crackers, 145

Savory Cheddar and Herb
 Muffins, 99

Seven-Minute Icing, 180

Shortcake Biscuits, 152

S'mores Bars, 52

Snickerdoodle
 Cupcakes, 120

Snickerdoodles, 23

Soft Molasses Cookies, 28

Spiced Hot Chocolate
 Cookies, 35

Spicy Chili Crackers, 147
Stabilized Whipped
    Cream, 179
Strawberry Bread, 103
Strawberry-Rhubarb
    Galette, 82
Summer Peach Crumb
    Cake, 128
Summer Vegetable
    Tart, 89–90
Sweet Hawaiian
    Rolls, 155
Swiss Meringue
    Buttercream, 181
Vanilla Buttercream, 176
Vanilla Cupcakes, 114
Vanilla Layer Cake, 132
White Sandwich
    Bread, 163
Zucchini Bread, 100
Nuts, 7
    Apple-Walnut Cake, 130
    Banana Bread, 101
    Carrot Cake and
        Oatmeal Cookie
        Sandwiches, 40–41
    Chocolate Pecan Pie, 63
    Fudgy Chocolate
        Brownies, 47
    Hummingbird Layer
        Cake, 136
    No-Knead Cranberry-Pecan
        Bread, 160–161
    Pecan Pie Bars, 54
    Pistachio Cookies, 32
    Praline Pumpkin
        Pie, 68–69

O

Oatmeal Chocolate Chip
    Cookie Bars, 51
Oatmeal Cookies, 30
Oats
    Apple Pie Bars, 55
    Carrot Cake and
        Oatmeal Cookie
        Sandwiches, 40–41
    Cranberry-Pear Crumble
        Pie, 65
    Monster Cookies, 36
    Oatmeal Chocolate Chip
        Cookie Bars, 51
    Oatmeal Cookies, 30
    Raspberry Jam Bars, 56
Olive Oil Flatbread
    Crackers, 144
Oranges
    Cranberry-Orange
        Bread, 105
    Glazed Orange Ricotta
        Cookies, 39
    Irish Soda Bread, 108
    Orange Muffins, 97
    Orange Pound Cake, 125
    Orange Sweet Rolls,
        156–157

P

Parchment paper, 5
Peaches
    Maple-Peach Bars, 49
    Peach-Blueberry
        Tart, 86
    Summer Peach Crumb
        Cake, 128

Peanut butter
    Black Bottom Peanut
        Butter Mousse Pie,
        74–75
    Monster Cookies, 36
    Peanut Butter
        Cupcakes, 118
    Soft Peanut Butter
        Cookies, 29
Pecan Pie Bars, 54
Perfect Chocolate Chip
    Cookies, 31
Pie dish, 4
Pies. *See also* Galettes;
    Quiches; Tarts
    Apple Streusel Pie, 64
    Banana Cream Pie,
        76–77
    Blueberry Crumble
        Pie, 66–67
    Brownie Pie, 62
    Chocolate Cream
        Pie, 72–73
    Chocolate Pecan Pie, 63
    Coconut Cream Pie,
        78–79
    Cranberry-Pear Crumble
        Pie, 65
    Fresh Cherry Pie, 70–71
    Key Lime Pie, 61
    Lemon Meringue
        Pie, 80–81
    Praline Pumpkin
        Pie, 68–69
Pineapple
    Hummingbird Layer
        Cake, 136

Pineapple Upside-Down
Cake, 131
Pistachio Cookies, 32
Powdered Sugar Glaze, 170
Praline Pumpkin Pie, 68–69
Preparation techniques, 7–9
Pumpkin purée
Praline Pumpkin Pie, 68–69
Pumpkin and White
Chocolate Chip
Cookies, 33
Pumpkin Bars, 48
Pumpkin Cake, 124

Q
Quiches
Bacon and Swiss Quiche, 91
Mushroom Quiche, 92
Sausage and Spinach
Quiche, 93
Quick breads
Banana Bread, 101
Cheesy Beer Bread, 106
Cinnamon Swirl Bread
(quick bread), 110
Coconut Bread, 102
Cranberry-Orange
Bread, 105
Double Chocolate Chip
Bread, 109
Honey Cornbread, 107
Irish Soda Bread, 108
Lemon and Poppy Seed
Bread, 104
Strawberry Bread, 103
Zucchini Bread, 100

R
Raisins
Carrot Cake and
Oatmeal Cookie
Sandwiches, 40–41
Irish Soda Bread, 108
Oatmeal Cookies, 30
Raspberry-Almond
Thumbprints, 24
Raspberry Cheesecake
Brownies, 57
Raspberry Jam Bars, 56
Red Velvet Chocolate Chip
Cookies, 37
Red Velvet Layer Cake, 134
Rhubarb-Strawberry
Galette, 82
Ricotta Orange Cookies,
Glazed, 39
Rolling pins, 4
Rolls
Knotted Herb-Garlic
Dinner Rolls, 166–167
Orange Sweet Rolls,
156–157
Sweet Hawaiian Rolls, 155

S
Salt, 7
Saltine Crackers, 145
Sausage and Spinach
Quiche, 93
Savory Cheddar and Herb
Muffins, 99
Scones
Apple-Cinnamon
Scones, 153

Maple-Bacon Scones, 154
Seven-Minute Icing, 180
Shortcake Biscuits, 152
Shortening, 6
Silicone baking mats, 5
S'mores Bars, 52
Snickerdoodle Cupcakes, 120
Snickerdoodles, 23
Soft Molasses Cookies, 28
Soft Peanut Butter
Cookies, 29
Sour cream
Banana Bread, 101
Banana Cupcakes, 117
Chocolate Cupcakes, 115
Key Lime Pie, 61
Lemon and Poppy Seed
Bread, 104
Mushroom Quiche, 92
Orange Pound Cake, 125
Spiced Hot Chocolate
Cookies, 35
Spicy Chili Crackers, 147
Spinach and Sausage
Quiche, 93
Stabilized Whipped
Cream, 179
Stand mixers, 5
Strawberry Bread, 103
Strawberry-Rhubarb
Galette, 82
Sugars, 5–6
creaming with butter, 13
measuring, 8
Summer Peach Crumb
Cake, 128

Summer Vegetable
  Tart, 89–90
Sweet Hawaiian Rolls, 155
Swiss Meringue
  Buttercream, 181

T

Tart pan, 4
Tarts
  Berry White Chocolate
    Tart, 88
  Lemon Cheesecake Tart, 87
  Peach-Blueberry Tart, 86
  Summer Vegetable
    Tart, 89–90
Techniques
  baking, 12–16
  preparation, 7–9
Tomatoes
  Caprese Galette, 85
Tools, 4–5

U

Utensils, 4–5

V

Vanilla Buttercream, 176
Vanilla Cupcakes, 114
Vanilla Layer Cake, 132

W

Whipped cream
  Banana Cream Pie, 76–77
  Chocolate Cream
    Pie, 72–73
  Coconut Cream Pie, 78–79
  Stabilized Whipped
    Cream, 179
Whipping egg whites, 15
White chocolate
  Berry White Chocolate
    Tart, 88
  Cookies and Cream
    Bars, 45

Pistachio Cookies, 32
Pumpkin and White
  Chocolate Chip
  Cookies, 33
White Sandwich Bread, 163
Whole-Wheat Biscuits, 150
Whole-Wheat Crackers, 142

Y

Yeast, 6
Yogurt, Greek
  Blueberry-Lemon Coffee
  Cake, 129

Z

Zucchini
  Chocolate Zucchini
  Cake, 127
  Summer Vegetable
  Tart, 89–90
Zucchini Bread, 100

About The Author

 *Heather Perine* is a teacher, recipe developer, and food blogger. Originally a farm girl from upstate New York, she now resides outside of Boston with her husband, Jason, and her black lab, Mila. She blogs about baking from scratch and shares easy dessert recipes at BostonGirlBakes.com.

CPSIA information can be obtained
at www.ICGtesting.com
Printed in the USA
BVHW060556250121
598470BV00008B/8